COMMON CORE
LANGUAGE ARTS
4Today

**Daily
Skill Practice**

Grade 3

Carson-Dellosa Publishing, LLC
Greensboro, North Carolina

Credits

Content Editors: Nancy Rogers Bosse and Christine Schwab
Copy Editor: Karen Seberg

Visit *carsondellosa.com* for correlations to Common Core State, national, and Canadian provincial standards.

Carson-Dellosa Publishing, LLC
PO Box 35665
Greensboro, NC 27425 USA
carsondellosa.com

ISBN 978-1-62442-606-3

Table of Contents

Common Core Language Arts 4 Today: Daily Skill Practice is a perfect supplement to any classroom language arts curriculum. Students' reading skills will grow as they work on comprehension, fluency, vocabulary, and decoding. Students' writing skills will improve as they work on elements of writing, writing structure, genre, parts of speech, grammar, and spelling, as well as the writing process.

This book covers 40 weeks of daily practice. Four comprehension questions or writing exercises a day for four days a week will provide students with ample practice in language arts skills. A separate assessment is included for the fifth day of each week.

Various skills and concepts are reinforced throughout the book through activities that align to the Common Core State Standards. To view these standards, please see the Common Core State Standards Alignment Matrix on pages 7 and 8.

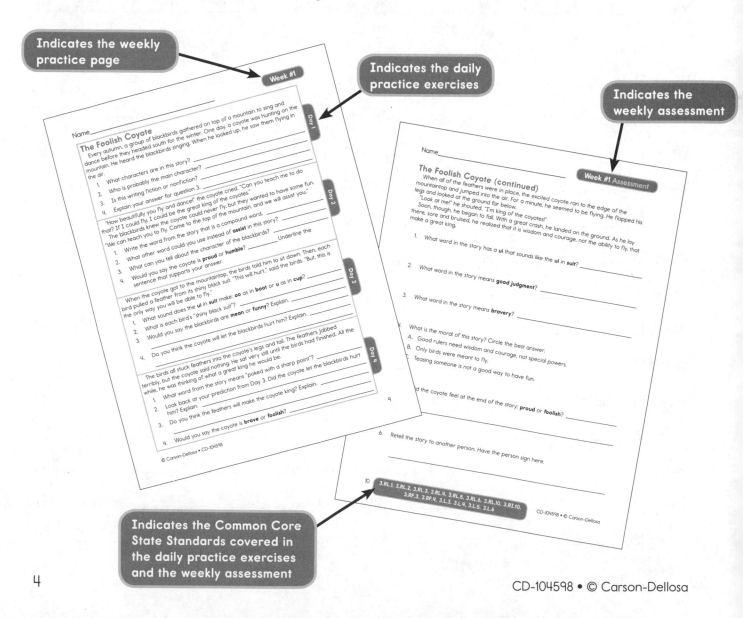

Indicates the weekly practice page

Indicates the daily practice exercises

Indicates the weekly assessment

Indicates the Common Core State Standards covered in the daily practice exercises and the weekly assessment

Building a Reading Environment

A positive reading environment is essential to fostering successful readers. When building a reading environment, think of students' physical, emotional, and cognitive needs.

Physical Environment
- Make the physical reading environment inviting and comfortable. Create a reading corner with comfortable chairs, floor pillows, a rug, enticing lighting, etc.
- Give students access to a variety of texts by providing books, magazines, newspapers, and Internet access. Read signs, ads, posters, menus, pamphlets, labels, boxes, and more!
- Provide regularly scheduled independent reading time in class. Encourage students to read at home. They can read to a younger sibling or read anything of interest such as comic books, children's and sports magazines, chapter books, etc.
- Set a positive example. Make sure students see you reading too!

Emotional Environment
- Learn about students' reading habits, preferences, strengths, and weaknesses. Then, provide books that address these issues.
- Help students create connections with text. Facilitate connections by activating prior knowledge, examining personal meaning, and respecting personal reflections.
- Give students the opportunity to choose titles to read. This will give them a sense of ownership, which will engage them in the text and sustain interest.
- Create a safe environment for exploring and trying new things. Foster a feeling of mutual respect for reading abilities and preferences.
- Require students to read at an appropriate reading level. Text in any content area, including leisure reading, should not be too easy or too difficult.
- Have all students participate in reading, regardless of their reading levels. Try to include slower readers and be sure to give them time to finish before moving on or asking questions.
- Be enthusiastic about reading! Talk about books you love and share your reading experiences and habits. Your attitude about reading is contagious!

Cognitive Environment
- Regardless of the grade level, read aloud to students every day. Reading aloud not only provides a good example but also lets students practice their listening skills.
- Help students build their vocabularies to make their reading more successful. Create word walls, personal word lists, mini-dictionaries, and graphic organizers.
- Read for different purposes. Reading a novel requires different skills than reading an instruction manual. Teach students the strategies needed to comprehend these different texts.
- Encourage students to talk about what and how they read. Use journal writing, literature circles, class discussions, conferences, conversations, workshops, seminars, and more.
- Writing and reading are inherently linked. Students can examine their own writing through reading and examine their reading skills by writing. Whenever possible, facilitate the link between reading and writing.

Choose a **topic** for your writing.
- What am I writing about?

Decide on a **purpose** for writing.
- Why am I writing this piece?
- What do I hope the audience will learn from reading this piece?

Identify your **audience**.
- Whom am I writing to?

Decide on a writing **style**.
- Expository—gives information or explains facts or ideas
- Persuasive—tries to talk someone into something
- Narrative—tells a story
- Descriptive—presents a clear picture of a person, place, thing, or idea

Decide on a **genre**—essay, letter, poetry, autobiography, fiction, or nonfiction.

Decide on a **point of view**—first person, second person, or third person.

Brainstorm by listing or drawing your main ideas.

Use a graphic organizer to **organize** your thoughts.

Revise, revise, revise!
- Use **descriptive words**.
- Use **transitions** and linking expressions.
- Use a **variety of sentence structures**.
- **Elaborate** with facts and details.
- Group your ideas into **paragraphs**.
- **Proofread** for capitalization, punctuation, and spelling.

Common Core State Standards Alignment Matrix

STANDARD	W1	W2	W3	W4	W5	W6	W7	W8	W9	W10	W11	W12	W13	W14	W15	W16	W17	W18	W19	W20
3.RL.1	●		●		●		●		●		●		●		●		●			
3.RL.2	●		●				●		●		●		●		●		●			
3.RL.3	●		●				●		●		●		●		●		●			
3.RL.4	●		●		●		●		●		●		●		●		●			
3.RL.5	●		●		●		●		●		●		●		●		●			
3.RL.6	●		●				●		●				●		●		●			
3.RL.7											●									
3.RL.9											●		●		●		●			
3.RL.10	●		●		●		●		●		●		●		●		●			
3.RI.1			●		●		●				●								●	
3.RI.2			●		●		●				●								●	
3.RI.3							●												●	
3.RI.4			●				●												●	
3.RI.5			●																●	
3.RI.6																				
3.RI.7											●									
3.RI.8											●									
3.RI.9							●				●								●	
3.RI.10	●		●		●		●												●	
3.RF.3	●		●		●		●		●		●		●		●		●		●	
3.RF.4	●		●		●		●		●		●		●		●		●		●	
3.W.1																				
3.W.2												●								●
3.W.3														●						
3.W.4													●	●						●
3.W.5													●	●						●
3.W.6													●	●						●
3.W.7																				
3.W.8																				
3.W.10													●	●						
3.L.1		●		●		●		●		●			●			●		●		●
3.L.2		●		●		●		●		●			●			●		●		●
3.L.3	●		●		●		●		●		●		●		●		●		●	
3.L.4	●		●		●		●		●		●		●		●		●			
3.L.5	●		●		●		●		●		●		●		●		●			
3.L.6	●		●		●		●		●		●		●		●		●			

W = Week

STANDARD	W21	W22	W23	W24	W25	W26	W27	W28	W29	W30	W31	W32	W33	W34	W35	W36	W37	W38	W39	W40
3.RL.1					●				●											
3.RL.2					●				●											
3.RL.3					●				●											
3.RL.4					●				●											
3.RL.5					●				●											
3.RL.6									●											
3.RL.7																				
3.RL.9					●															
3.RL.10					●															
3.RI.1	●		●		●		●		●		●		●		●		●		●	
3.RI.2	●		●		●		●		●		●	●	●	●	●		●		●	
3.RI.3	●		●		●		●		●		●		●		●		●		●	
3.RI.4	●		●		●		●		●				●		●				●	
3.RI.5	●				●															
3.RI.6	●		●				●		●				●		●		●		●	
3.RI.7							●													
3.RI.8					●		●		●		●		●		●		●		●	
3.RI.9	●				●				●											
3.RI.10	●		●		●		●		●				●		●		●		●	
3.RF.3	●		●		●		●		●		●									
3.RF.4	●		●		●		●		●		●									
3.W.1		●																		
3.W.2				●		●		●					●		●		●	●		
3.W.3																				●
3.W.4		●		●		●		●				●		●			●		●	●
3.W.5		●		●		●		●				●		●			●		●	●
3.W.6		●		●		●		●				●		●			●		●	●
3.W.7																		●		●
3.W.8																		●		●
3.W.10		●		●				●				●		●		●		●		
3.L.1		●		●		●		●		●		●		●			●			●
3.L.2		●		●		●		●		●		●	●	●	●	●	●	●	●	●
3.L.3		●		●		●	●	●	●			●	●	●	●	●	●			●
3.L.4					●		●		●				●		●		●		●	
3.L.5					●		●		●				●		●		●		●	
3.L.6					●		●		●				●		●		●		●	

W = Week

8

Name_____

The Foolish Coyote

Day 1

Every autumn, a group of blackbirds gathered on top of a mountain to sing and dance before they headed south for the winter. One day, a coyote was hunting on the mountain. He heard the blackbirds singing. When he looked up, he saw them flying in the air.

1. What characters are in this story? _____

2. Who is probably the main character? _____

3. Is this writing fiction or nonfiction? _____

4. Explain your answer for question 3. _____

Day 2

"How beautifully you fly and dance!" the coyote cried. "Can you teach me to do that? If I could fly, I could be the great king of the coyotes."

The blackbirds knew the coyote could never fly, but they wanted to have some fun. "We can teach you to fly. Come to the top of the mountain, and we will assist you."

1. Write the word from the story that is a compound word. _____

2. What other word could you use instead of **assist** in this story? _____

3. What can you tell about the character of the blackbirds? _____

4. Would you say the coyote is **proud** or **humble**? _____ Underline the sentence that supports your answer.

Day 3

When the coyote got to the mountaintop, the birds told him to sit down. Then, each bird pulled a feather from its shiny black suit. "This will hurt," said the birds. "But, this is the only way you will be able to fly."

1. What sound does the **ui** in **suit** make: **oo** as in **boot** or **u** as in **cup**? _____

2. What is each bird's "shiny black suit"? _____

3. Would you say the blackbirds are **mean** or **funny**? Explain. _____

_____

4. Do you think the coyote will let the blackbirds hurt him? Explain. _____

_____

Day 4

The birds all stuck feathers into the coyote's legs and tail. The feathers jabbed terribly, but the coyote said nothing. He sat very still until the birds had finished. All the while, he was thinking of what a great king he would be.

1. What word from the story means "poked with a sharp point"? _____

2. Look back at your prediction from Day 3. Did the coyote let the blackbirds hurt him? Explain. _____

3. Do you think the feathers will make the coyote king? Explain. _____

_____

4. Would you say the coyote is **brave** or **foolish**? _____

The Foolish Coyote (continued)

When all of the feathers were in place, the excited coyote ran to the edge of the mountaintop and jumped into the air. For a minute, he seemed to be flying. He flapped his legs and looked at the ground far below.

"Look at me!" he shouted. "I'm king of the coyotes!"

Soon, though, he began to fall. With a great crash, he landed on the ground. As he lay there, sore and bruised, he realized that it is wisdom and courage, not the ability to fly, that make a great king.

1. What word in the story has a **ui** that sounds like the **ui** in **suit**? _____

2. What word in the story means **good judgment**? _____

3. What word in the story means **bravery**? _____

4. What is the moral of this story? Circle the best answer.

    A. Good rulers need wisdom and courage, not special powers.

    B. Only birds were meant to fly.

    C. Teasing someone is not a good way to have fun.

5. How did the coyote feel at the end of the story: **proud** or **foolish**? _____

    Explain. _____

6. Retell the story to another person. Have the person sign here.

    _____

3.RL.1, 3.RL.2, 3.RL.3, 3.RL.4, 3.RL.5, 3.RL.6, 3.RL.10, 3.RI.10, 3.RF.3, 3.RF.4, 3.L.3, 3.L.4, 3.L.5, 3.L.6   CD-104598 • © Carson-Dellosa

Name_____

Rewrite the story title with the correct capital letters.
1. "a night in the desert" _____

Write **a** if the word begins with a consonant sound. Write **an** if the word begins with a vowel sound.
2. _____ daisy   _____ iris

Write the missing commas in the sentence.
3. Fleas flies and fish are fantastic frog food.

Read the plural nouns. Write the matching singular nouns.
4. mice _____   octopi _____

Rewrite the story title with the correct capital letters.
1. "watch out!" _____

Write **a** if the word begins with a consonant sound. Write **an** if the word begins with a vowel sound.
2. _____ zinnia   _____ forget-me-not

Write the missing commas in the sentence.
3. Pilar picks petunias peonies and pansies.

Read the plural nouns. Write the matching singular nouns.
4. men _____   fungi _____

Rewrite the story title with the correct capital letters.
1. "rudy's rowdy robots" _____

Write **a** if the word begins with a consonant sound. Write **an** if the word begins with a vowel sound.
2. _____ lilac   _____ Indian paintbrush

Write the missing commas in the sentence.
3. Does Ivan live in Illinois Idaho or Iowa?

Read the plural nouns. Write the matching singular nouns.
4. children _____   tomatoes _____

Rewrite the story title with the correct capital letters.
1. "i am not a penguin" _____

Write **a** if the word begins with a consonant sound. Write **an** if the word begins with a vowel sound.
2. _____ orange blossom   _____ apple blossom

Write the missing commas in the sentence.
3. Joanna jumps jogs and juggles.

Read the plural nouns. Write the matching singular nouns.
4. wolves _____   heroes _____

Rewrite the story titles with the correct capital letters.

1. "cars, trains, bikes, and planes" _____

2. "the worst day of my life" _____

Write **a** if the word begins with a consonant sound. Write **an** if the word begins with a vowel sound.

3. _____ magnolia blossom   _____ azalea

4. _____ petunia   _____ impatiens

5. _____ orchid   _____ water lily

Write the missing commas in the sentences.

6. Julio is shopping for pens pencils and erasers.

7. Mia is taking a trip to Washington Oregon and California.

8. John Dion and Miguel are going to the skate park.

Read the plural nouns. Write the matching singular nouns.

9. geese _____   men _____

10. brushes _____   shelves _____

Name_____

Navajo Hogans

The Navajo tribes lived in the Southwestern United States. Their homes, called **hogans**, were made of wood and mud and were built in different shapes. Some hogans were shaped like a dome. Others were shaped like a hexagon or an octagon.

1. Which word in this paragraph is a compound word? _____

2. What is a **hogan**? _____

3. Underline the sentence that is the main idea of this paragraph.

4. List one detail that supports the main idea. _____

Day 1

While the shape of the hogans could vary, some characteristics of the houses were always the same. The hogan was built so that the door faced east. This way, the morning rays of the sun shone inside the house. The Navajo believed that the sun brought ideas and planning.

1. Write the word that has a silent **gh**. _____

2. What is the opposite of **always**? _____

3. Underline the sentence that is the main idea of this paragraph.

4. List one detail that supports the main idea. _____

_____

Day 2

Hogans were constructed with four mighty posts to hold up the roof. The posts had special meanings. The post on the north side of the house stood for confidence. The post to the east represented thinking. The south post meant planning. The post to the west stood for life.

1. Write the word that has a silent **gh**. _____

2. What are two other words for **represented**? _____

3. Underline the sentence that is the main idea of this paragraph.

4. List two details that support the main idea. _____

_____

Day 3

After a house was built, the Navajo blessed the house. A person was chosen to stand at the door and walk clockwise past each post. They hoped for a life in which they lived as one with nature.

1. Which word in this paragraph is a compound word? _____

2. What is the opposite of **clockwise**?
   A. unclockwise   B. counterclockwise

3. Underline the sentence that is the main idea of this paragraph.

4. List one detail that supports the main idea. _____

_____

Day 4

Why Bats Fly at Night

Long ago, the earthbound animals and the birds fought long battles each day. The bat would sit in a tree to see which group would win. If wings were clapping and beaks were cheering, the bat flew to their side. "I have wings, so I belong with you," he would say.

But, if the earthbound animals with their sharp teeth and claws were winning, the bat would quickly fly to their side. "I'm glad I'm fighting with you," the bat would say.

The animals stared at the bat. "You are not an animal because you have wings," said the bear.

The bat smiled and showed his sharp teeth. "I may have wings, but no bird has teeth like this," he said. The animals agreed, and the bat sat with them.

After a while, the birds and animals got tired of their battles. They met with the chiefs to settle their differences. The wise chiefs knew what the bat had done.

"Bat, you have not been a friend to either the birds or the animals," the chiefs said. "You will live alone and fly only at nighttime when all of the animals and birds sleep." And, that explains why bats fly at night and live alone.

1. List all of the words that have a **silent gh**. _____

   _____

   Which one is a compound word? _____

2. What word in the story is the opposite of **foolish**? _____

3. How would you describe the bat?

   A. sneaky   B. trustworthy   C. a good friend

4. What is this story mainly about?

   A. why bats have wings

   B. why earthbound animals and birds do not live together

   C. why bats fly at night

5. Turn your answer to question 4 into a sentence.

   _____ because _____

   _____ .

 3.RL.1, 3.RL.2, 3.RL.3, 3.RL.4, 3.RL.5, 3.RL.6, 3.RL.10, 3.RI.1, 3.RI.2, 3.RI.4, 3.RI.5, 3.RI.10, 3.RF.3, 3.RF.4, 3.L.3, 3.L.4, 3.L.5, 3.L.6   CD-104598 • © Carson-Dellosa

Correct the capitalization errors.
1.   alex goes to soccer practice on tuesdays and thursdays.

Circle the correct verb.
2.   Isabella (drink, drinks) milk with her dinner.

Add an apostrophe where it is needed.
3.   The trees leaves were thick and green.

Look at the picture. Circle the correct plural noun.
4.   monkeys   monkies

Correct the capitalization errors.
1.   we celebrate the fourth of july by boating on the lake.

Circle the correct verb.
2.   Ana (bake, bakes) cookies with her mother.

Add an apostrophe where it is needed.
3.   The squirrels fur was soft and gray.

Look at the picture. Circle the correct plural noun.
4.   partys   parties

Correct the capitalization errors.
1.   jenna's dance recital is on valentine's day.

Circle the correct verb.
2.   Dad (drives, drive) me to school.

Add an apostrophe where it is needed.
3.   The small dogs leash dragged on the ground as he ran.

Look at the picture. Circle the correct plural noun.
4.   babys   babies

Correct the capitalization errors.
1.   kelly went to ellen's house on friday.

Circle the correct verb that completes the sentence.
2.   Edgar and his brother (share, shares) a bedroom.

Add an apostrophe where it is needed.
3.   The childrens ball rolled into the street.

Look at the picture. Circle the correct plural noun.
4.   turkeys   turkies

Name_____

Correct the capitalization errors.

1. my sister will be six years old in may.

2. in january, we always go sledding on saturday mornings.

3. jamie's favorite holiday is hanukkah, which comes in december.

Circle the correct verbs.

4. Our team (wear, wears) red uniforms.
5. My grandparents (live, lives) next door.

Add apostrophes where they are needed.

6. Brads favorite food is pizza.
7. The birds nest was made of mud and twigs.
8. My dads car is dark green.

Look at the pictures. Circle the correct plural nouns.

9.

valleys   vallies

10.

storys   stories

Name_____

How Wolves Communicate

Wolves, the wild relatives of dogs, live in family groups. Scientists have found that wolves communicate, or talk, to each other with howls, noises, and movements. The wolves use their voices and their bodies to tell each other important information.

1. Does **howls** rhyme with **owls** or **bowls**? _____

2. What other word for **talk** is used in this paragraph? _____

3. Does the **mu** in **communicate** sound more like **mew** or **moo**? _____

4. What do wolves use to communicate? _____

Day 1

Wolves howl to tell other wolves to stay away. They may also howl to call each other back to the pack. A wolf may snarl or growl if danger is near or another wolf is threatening. Wolves may bark a warning or a challenge.

1. List the two **ow** words that rhyme. _____

2. What does it mean if a wolf "barks a challenge"? _____

3. Write the different wolf sounds. _____

4. List four different ways humans communicate. _____

_____

Day 2

When one wolf wants to tell another he is the boss, he will keep his head high and ears forward. His tail will also be held high, but not wagging. He will stare directly at the wolf with which he is communicating and keep his mouth relaxed.

1. Is the **a** in **relaxed** a **short a** or a **long a**? _____

2. What is the opposite of **forward**? _____

3. What does it mean to be "the boss"? _____

4. Which parts of the wolf are held high when he wants to tell another wolf he is the boss? _____

Day 3

When a wolf wants to play, she looks much like a playful dog. The wolf will go down on her front paws with her tail in the air like she is bowing. The tail will wag. The wolf will be smiling with her tongue hanging out.

1. Which word has a **long a** and a suffix that means **full of**? _____

2. When a tail **wags,** it goes   A. back and forth.   B. up and down.

3. How do you act when you want to play? _____

4. A wolf is smiling, and her tail is high and wagging. What does that mean? _____

_____

Day 4

Hopi Poem
by Anonymous

Come here, Thunder, and look!
Come here, Cold, and see it rain!
Thunder strikes and makes it hot.
All seeds grow when it is hot.
Corn in blossom,
Beans in blossom,
Your face on gardens looks,
Watermelon plant, muskmelon plant.
Your face on gardens looks.
Aha-aha-ehe-ihe

1. List the three words in this poem that have the **long a** sound. _____

    _____

2. Is **muskmelon** a meat or a fruit? _____

    How can you tell? _____

3. There are three phrases that the poet repeats twice each. List them.

    _____

    _____

    _____

4. In the poem, what makes the ground hot? _____

5. Personification is a literary tool used to give nonhuman things human qualities. Write
    how thunder is personified in this poem. _____

    _____

    _____

3.RL.1, 3.RL.4, 3.RL.5, 3.RL.10, 3.RI.1, 3.RI.2, 3.RI.10, 3.RF.3, 3.RF.4, 3.L.3, 3.L.4, 3.L.5, 3.L.6   CD-104598 • © Carson-Dellosa

Name_____

Rewrite the song title with the correct capital letters.
1. "how much is that doggie in the window?" _____

_____

Circle the helping verb in the sentence. Underline the main verb.
2. Next week, I will sing in the school talent show.

Add commas to the sentence if they are needed.
3. My mother grows roses daisies and violets in her garden.

Write **your** or **you're** to correctly complete the sentence.
4. _____ invited to my sleepover.

Rewrite the book title with the correct capital letters.
1. *the biography of helen keller* _____

Circle the helping verb in the sentence. Underline the main verb.
2. Someday, I will teach my dog to fetch.

Add commas to the sentence if they are needed.
3. My brother's name is John Henry Foster.

Write **your** or **you're** to correctly complete the sentence.
4. Please bring _____ sleeping bag.

Rewrite the magazine title with the correct capital letters.
1. *ranger rick* _____

Circle the helping verb in the sentence. Underline the main verb.
2. After school, Carter can come to my house.

Add commas to the sentence if they are needed.
3. There are maple pine oak and elm trees on my street.

Write **your** or **you're** to correctly complete the sentence.
4. _____ welcome to bring your dog.

Rewrite the book title with the correct capital letters.
1. *green eggs and ham* _____

Circle the helping verb in the sentence. Underline the main verb.
2. Can you watch the movie with me tonight?

Add commas to the sentence if they are needed.
3. We study spelling math history and art in my class.

Write **your** or **you're** to correctly complete the sentence.
4. _____ mom will drive you to my house.

Name_____

Rewrite the titles with the correct capital letters.

1. "twinkle, twinkle, little star" _____

2. *the big book of lizards* _____

Circle the helping verbs in the sentences. Underline the main verbs.

3. Amy will write her report after class.

4. The bird can fly now that her wing is healed.

5. The sun will rise tomorrow.

Add commas to the sentences if they are needed.

6. Claire Philip Tara Jose and I went to the movies together.

7. Tara brought her dogs Peaches Romeo and Clyde to the park.

8. Mischa's favorite colors are yellow purple blue and pink.

Write **your** or **you're** to correctly complete the sentences.

9. You have to call _____ parents.

10. _____ going to love my new game!

20 **3.L.1, 3.L.2**

Cherry Blossom Time

Japan has a holiday just for girls and a holiday just for boys. But, Japan has holidays for the whole family too. April is the month for the Cherry Blossom Festival. It is a holiday for the whole family.

1. What country is this passage talking about? _____

2. What time of year is this passage about? _____

3. Will people celebrate the Cherry Blossom Festival inside or outside? _____
   Why? _____

4. What holidays does your family celebrate? _____

Day 1

Cherry trees have flowers for only one week. During that week, everyone goes to look at the trees. Entire families go to the park together and stay all day. They take a picnic lunch in a box called an "obentou." At the park, they eat lunch under the cherry trees. They sing songs and tell stories.

1. Where do people go to enjoy cherry blossom time? _____

2. How long is cherry blossom time? _____

3. If your family was in Japan, whom would you go to the festival with? _____

4. How long do you think most people will stay at the park? _____

Day 2

Everyone stays at the park until after dark. The cherry trees are prettiest at night. The whole sky is filled with pink cherry blossoms. People stay up late at night to see the flowers because they know the flowers will be gone soon.

1. How late do people stay at the park? _____

2. According to this passage, when are the cherry trees prettiest? _____

3. Would you stay up late to see the cherry blossoms? _____

4. How do you think the people will feel at the end of the festival? _____

   _____

Day 3

The end of the Cherry Blossom Festival is a sad time. All of the pretty flowers are gone. But, the people know the cherry trees will bloom next year.

1. What do the cherry trees look like at the end of the festival? _____

2. When will the next Cherry Blossom Festival be? _____

3. Why are people sad at the end of this festival? _____

4. What could you say to cheer up the sad people? _____

   _____

Day 4

Name_____

Rain in Summer
by Henry Wadsworth Longfellow

How beautiful is the rain!
After the dust and heat,
In the broad and fiery street,
In the narrow lane,
How beautiful is the rain!

How it clatters along the roofs,
Like the tramp of hoofs!
How it gushes and struggles out
From the throat of the overflowing spout!

Across the window-pane
It pours and pours;
And swift and wide,
With a muddy tide,
Like a river down the gutter roars
The rain, the welcome rain!

1. List the words in the poem that rhyme with **rain**. _____

2. Is the sound **clatter** more like a **rattle** or a **hum**? _____

3. How does the author feel about rain? _____
    _____

    How can you tell he feels this way? _____
    _____

4. How do you feel about rain? _____

5. Why did the poet write this poem?
    A. to tell how rain feels
    B. to express how much he likes rain
    C. to give facts about rain

3.RL.1, 3.RL.2, 3.RL.3, 3.RL.4, 3.RL.5, 3.RL.6, 3.RL.10, 3.RI.1, 3.RI.2, 3.RI.3, 3.RI.4, 3.RI.9, 3.RI.10, 3.RF.3, 3.RF.4, 3.L.3, 3.L.4, 3.L.5, 3.L.6

Day 1

Correct the capitalization errors.
1.   have you ever seen a painting of a huge flower?

Circle the correct adjective.
2.   The summer solstice is the (longer, longest) day of the year.

Add the missing apostrophes. Then, write the two words that make up each contraction.
3.   isnt _____   shouldnt _____

Read the singular nouns. Write the matching plural nouns.
4.   woman _____   potato _____

Day 2

Correct the capitalization errors.
1.   the painting may have been done by georgia o'Keeffe.

Circle the correct adjective.
2.   Which instrument is the (louder, loudest) in the band?

Add the missing apostrophes. Then, write the two words that make up each contraction.
3.   couldnt _____   arent _____

Read the singular nouns. Write the matching plural nouns.
4.   half _____   echo _____

Day 3

Correct the capitalization errors.
1.   even as a young girl, georgia knew that she wanted to be an artist.

Circle the correct adjective.
2.   January is usually (colder, coldest) than July.

Add the missing apostrophes. Then, write the two words that make up each contraction.
3.   wasnt _____   didnt _____

Read the singular nouns. Write the matching plural nouns.
4.   shelf _____   deer _____

Day 4

Correct the capitalization errors.
1.   Georgia o'keeffe was born on a farm in wisconsin in 1887.

Circle the correct adjective.
2.   Your piece of pie is (larger, largest) than mine.

Add the missing apostrophes. Then, write the two words that make up each contraction.
3.   dont _____   werent _____

Read the singular nouns. Write the matching plural nouns.
4.   goose _____   mouse _____

Name_____

Correct the capitalization errors.

1. Georgia O'keeffe went to art school in chicago and New york, and she taught art in texas.

2. she painted the things she loved—sky, flowers, mountains, and trees.

3. when she died at age 98, she was recognized as one of america's great artists.

Circle the correct adjectives.

4. Iesha is the (stronger, strongest) girl in third grade.
5. Cheetahs are (faster, fastest) than rabbits.
6. Quan is the (funnier, funniest) student in our class.

Add the missing apostrophes. Then, write the two words that make up each contraction.

7. cant _____   havent _____

8. wouldnt _____   wont _____

Read the singular nouns. Write the matching plural nouns.

9. monkey _____   half _____
10. goose _____   woman _____

March 15, 1405
Dear Father,
    I miss you and the family, but I am happy to be living here and serving Sir Stephen. Castle life is exciting, and I am learning the skills and behavior expected of a knight.

1. Whom is this story about, a **knight** or a **knight in training**? _____

2. Is this kind of writing a **poem** or a **letter**? _____

3. Whom is the author writing to? _____

4. Predict whether the rest of this letter will include details about a job the author finds **interesting** or **boring**. _____

    Many things are required of pages like me. My duties include taking care of Sir Stephen's horses and serving him as needed. I am also learning to spar with a sword and hunt with a falcon. I often play chess and other games that require great skill and strategy.

1. Whom does the author of this letter work for? _____

2. Underline five details that support the main idea in the first sentence.

3. Would you like to be a page? Explain. _____

4. Predict whether the author plans on **quitting** or **continuing** this job. _____
_____

    I can hardly wait seven years until I am 15; then, I can become a **squire**. A squire serves his master as a valet and is trained to become a mounted soldier. He also rides in battle with his master.

1. How old is the author? _____

2. How does he feel about becoming a squire? _____

3. What would you enjoy more, being a **squire** or a **page**? _____

4. Predict what squires do to test their battle skills. _____
_____

    The most exciting thing squires do is test their skill in a contest called jousting. In this contest, one squire tries to knock another squire off his horse with a long, blunt **lance**. Your faithful son,
Arthur

1. How do squires test their battle skills? _____

2. What do you think a **lance** is? _____

3. When could you see people jousting? _____

4. Did the author think a squire's job is **interesting** or **boring**? _____
Underline one detail from this paragraph that backs up your answer.

April 3, 1405
Dear Father,

I still miss you, but I have made some good friends. We are all quite busy working, learning, and serving Sir Stephen. My friend, Squire Robert, gets to help Sir Stephen put on his armor for contests.

Almost all parts of Sir Stephen's body are covered with his metal suit. When he is covered in armor, we cannot recognize him.

We can, however, recognize his coat of arms. It is a beautiful picture of a unicorn. This coat of arms is on Sir Stephen's shield, his horse's blanket, and his cloak.

I remain your faithful son,
Arthur

1. Who is the author of this letter, and to whom is he writing? _____

    _____

2. Besides the author, which other character helps Sir Stephen? _____

3. In this passage, what is **armor**? _____

4. Use clues from the passage to figure out what Sir Stephen's **coat of arms** looked like. Draw it below.

5. If you had a coat of arms, what would it look like? Draw it below.

Correct the capitalization errors.

1. mr. oliver sanchez
    1234 silver springs drive
    bangor, maine 04401

Write the correct past-tense form of the irregular verb.

2. Yesterday, the frogs _____ to the edge of the river.
    come

Add quotation marks around what a person said.

3. Jill won too medals, announced the coach.

4. If **two**, **to**, or **too** is used incorrectly in question 3, cross it out and write the correct word above it.

Day 1

Correct the capitalization errors.

1. mrs. hannah chadwick
    854 pine street
    garnet, montana 59770

Write the correct past-tense form of the irregular verb.

2. They _____ some little bugs.
    eat

Add quotation marks around what a person said.

3. Todd said, I like dogs to.

4. If **two**, **to**, or **too** is used incorrectly in question 3, cross it out and write the correct word above it.

Day 2

Correct the capitalization errors.

1. shelby peters
    347 sunshine lane
    davies, florida 32802

Write the correct past-tense form of the irregular verb.

2. One green frog _____ the big bugs on the other side.
    see

Add quotation marks around what a person said.

3. I'm going two walk to school, said Sue.

4. If **two**, **to**, or **too** is used incorrectly in question 3, cross it out and write the correct word above it.

Day 3

Correct the capitalization errors.

1. nathan avery
    72 tundra road
    barrow, alaska 99723

Write the correct past-tense form of the irregular verb.

2. He _____ that they could all cross the river.
    say

Add quotation marks around what a person said.

3. Hit the ball too me! Brian yelled.

4. If **two**, **to**, or **too** is used incorrectly in question 3, cross it out and write the correct word above it.

Day 4

Name_____

Correct the capitalization errors.

1. casey walsh

   298 center street

   littleton, maine 89764

2. tyrone hernandez

   10024 wells avenue

   claremont, california 91734

Write the correct past-tense forms of each irregular verb.

3. A yellow frog _____ to the pond and jumped in.
   come

4. He _____ a bunch of lily pads.
   see

5. He _____ the lily pads gave him an idea.
   say

Underline each sentence that includes a quote. Add quotation marks around what the person said.

6. Emma said that she likes apple pie.

   Apple pie is Emma's favorite dessert.

   I love apple pie, Emma told me.

7. I told Joey that I wanted to read his book.

   Joey said I could borrow his book.

   You will like this story, Joey said.

Read the sentences. If **two**, **to**, or **too** is used incorrectly, cross it out and write the correct word above it.

8. Two birds sang in the tree.

9. I think it is to cold outside.

10. Taneshia wants too go to the park.

Name_____

In the summer, many people go to lakes or rivers to fish. Fishing is a good sport in the summer. But, in the winter, the water is covered with ice. Some people think they cannot go fishing, but other people think that winter is a very good time to fish.

1. What time of year do most people go fishing?   A. summer   B. winter

2. What other time of year can people go fishing? _____

3. Where would people fish in winter? _____

4. Write a title to predict what activity this passage will describe. _____

_____

Day 1

How do people fish in the winter? They go ice fishing. Ice fishers put on warm clothes. Then, they find a lake that is covered with ice. The ice fishers walk out on the lake over the ice. The ice must be thick so that the fishers do not fall into the water.

1. Where do ice fishers go to fish? _____

2. What does the weather have to be like for safe ice fishing? _____

3. If you were going ice fishing, how would you keep warm? _____

4. Predict what the ice fishers will do once they are out on the ice. _____

_____

Day 2

Many ice fishers put up little houses on the ice. The houses help keep them warm. Then, the fishers cut a hole in the ice with an ax. They put their fishing lines into the water and wait for the fish to bite.

1. Where can ice fishers stay to keep warm? _____

2. Underline two things that may be found in an ice-fishing house.

3. Would you like to ice fish? Why? _____

4. Predict what an ice fisher does when a fish bites the line. _____

_____

Day 3

Many ice fishers use a machine called a "tip-up" to hold their lines. The tip-up makes a little flag pop up when a fish bites. Then, the fisher pulls the fish out of the water. Ice fishing is a cold sport. But, catching a big fish for dinner makes the cold feeling go away!

1. What machine holds the fishing lines for ice fishers? _____

2. What causes ice fishing to be a cold sport?
   A. characters   B. events   C. setting

3. How does a fisher know when a fish has bitten? _____

4. Look back at your prediction from Day 1. Did this passage describe the activity you predicted? Explain. _____

Day 4

29

Fishing for Sole

It was a cold, clear January morning. Jack stared out the window at the river behind his house. It had frozen over many weeks ago. Now, it was covered with thick ice. Suddenly, the phone rang. It was Grandpa Bill. "I need a fishing buddy, Jack. Do you know anyone who would be interested?"

"I sure do!" said Jack. "I'll meet you at the river in five minutes." Jack loved ice fishing with Grandpa Bill! Quickly, he put on several layers of warm clothes. He got his fishing line and headed down to the river. Grandpa Bill was already there with his ax, chopping at the thick ice. Soon, they each had a good-sized hole. With a *plop*, they dropped in their lines and waited.

Jack did not mind waiting. In fact, he liked spending time talking with his grandfather. Grandpa Bill had many interesting stories, and the time always passed quickly. Soon, Jack's tip-up flag popped up. He grabbed his fishing pole. He was so excited that he almost dropped the pole into the water!

Carefully, Jack pulled up his catch. He and his grandpa burst out laughing. It was not a fish at all. It was a huge boot! "That's OK," said Grandpa Bill. "I guess we're having 'sole' for dinner tonight, and I don't mean fish!"

1. Does the illustration help predict what the story will be about? Explain. _____

_____

2. What is the setting of the story? _____

_____

3. Describe how Jack feels about Grandpa Bill. _____

_____

4. What did Jack really catch? _____

5. How did your other passages this week help you understand this story?

_____

_____

 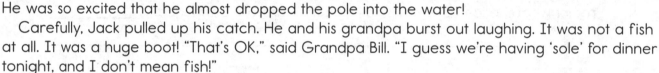

3.RL.1, 3.RL.2, 3.RL.3, 3.RL.4, 3.RL.5, 3.RL.7, 3.RL.9, 3.RL.10, 3.RI.1, 3.RI.2, 3.RI.7, 3.RI.8, 3.RI.9, 3.RF.3, 3.RF.4, 3.L.3, 3.L.4, 3.L.5, 3.L.6

CD-104598 • © Carson-Dellosa

Prewrite/Brainstorm

A paragraph is a group of sentences that tells the reader about one main idea. What is your favorite activity? To prepare to write a paragraph about your activity, write five words about your activity.

_____   _____   _____

_____   _____

Draft

Write a paragraph about your favorite activity. Use the five words you wrote to help you describe the activity. Be sure your paragraph has a main idea and at least three supporting ideas.

_____

_____

_____

_____

Revise

Read your paragraph about your favorite activity to an adult. Did you include all five words you used to describe it? Do they all support your main idea? Are the words in the right order? Are your word groups sentences? Rewrite your paragraph.

_____

_____

_____

_____

Proofread

Read your paragraph again. Do you see any capitalization errors? Are all of the words spelled correctly? Did you use the correct punctuation and grammar? Use proofreading marks to correct the sentences.

- ❑ Capitalization mistakes
- ❑ Grammar mistakes
- ❑ Punctuation mistakes
- ❑ Spelling mistakes

Publish

Write your final copy on a computer or on the lines below.
MAKE SURE it turns out

- NEAT—Make sure there are no wrinkles, creases, or holes.
- CLEAN—Erase any smudges or dirty spots.
- EASY TO READ—Use your best handwriting and good spacing between words.

_____

_____

_____

_____

_____

_____

_____

_____

_____

_____

_____

_____

_____

_____

3.W.2, 3.W.4, 3.W.5, 3.W.6, 3.W.10

Using Context Clues

Emily wears a long blue dress and a blue bonnet. Her head is made of china, and her shoes are real leather. Emily has lived with the same family for almost 200 years. But, her new owner is careless and forgetful.

1. Which word has a suffix that means **without**? _____

2. Is a **bonnet** a **hat** or a **shoe**? _____

3. What is Emily? _____

4. What is Emily's problem? _____

_____

Zack is white with black spots. He wears a red leather collar. He was trained to run to the truck whenever the alarm bell went off. He has just started a new life as a pet in the fire chief's family, but he is not happy. He misses fighting fires.

1. What sound does the **igh** in **fighting** make?
   A. **long i**   B. **ig** as in **pig**   C. **short i**

2. What other word could you use instead of **not happy**? _____

3. What is Zack's problem? _____

4. Where is Zack now? _____

James is homeless. His orange fur is matted, and his white paws are gray with mud. James is scared of people. He has found a house where a bowl of tuna fish sits on the step every morning.

1. Which word has a suffix that means **without**? _____

2. Is matted fur **tangled** or **fluffy**? _____

3. What is James's problem? _____

_____

4. How is James's problem solved? _____

_____

Shera lives in a place that used to have lots of trees. Now, people are building there. Shera is finding it harder and harder to find food. One night, she goes out hunting and flies into a big glass window.

1. What sound does the **igh** in **night** make?
   A. **long i**   B. **ig** as in **pig**   C. **short i**

2. Is an animal that hunts at night called **nocturnal** or **an early bird**?

_____

3. What is Shera's problem? _____

4. Where does this story take place?_____

Name_____

Everybody Has Problems

Read the three stories. Then, answer the questions.

Abigail hurried down the path. Sunlight fell through the red and yellow leaves. There was still frost on the fields. As Abigail came to the stone wall, she could hear the honking of geese. She wanted to stop to look for them, but she was late for school. Mrs. Lang had probably already given the spelling test, and there was no way she could make it up.

Kayla set her backpack on the rock. She wiped her face. It was very hot. The glare of the sun was hurting her eyes, and she was beginning to feel almost sightless. Everyone had told her not to hike in the desert at this time of year. Kayla looked toward the sun, which was starting to set. Then, she froze. She heard a rattling noise nearby.

Joseph's nose was bright red as he stomped into the house. He put his boots on the mat and set his mittens down to dry. Then, he saw that his backpack was open. His glasses were missing! It was too late to go look for them; it was already dark. He knew that Mom would not be able to buy him new ones. There was no money.

1. Circle the story words with an **igh** that makes the **long i** sound. Which of these words also has a suffix that means **without**? _____

2. If the sun is glaring, does that mean it is **bright** or **dim?** _____

3. Read each problem. Write the name of the person with the problem.

    A. I lost my glasses, and it is too dark to look for them. _____

    B. I was late for school and missed my spelling test. _____

    C. It is getting late, and I am alone in the desert with a rattlesnake. _____

4. Fill in the chart to show the time of day and time of year in each story.

Children	Time of Day	Time of Year
Abigail		
Kayla		
Joseph		

5. Which character do you think has the worst problem? _____
    Why? _____

 3.RL.1, 3.RL.2, 3.RL.3, 3.RL.4, 3.RL.5, 3.RL.6, 3.RL.9, 3.RL.10, 3.RF.3, 3.RF.4, 3.L.3, 3.L.4, 3.L.5, 3.L.6   CD-104598 • © Carson-Dellosa

Name_____

Prewrite/Brainstorm

Look at the picture.
What are the kids doing?
Fill in the chart with the
Five W's about the picture.

Who?	What?	Where?	When?	Why?

Draft

Write a summary about the picture. Use the Five W's to help you.

_____
_____
_____
_____
_____

Revise

Read your summary of the picture to an adult. Did you include all Five W's? Are the words in the right order? Are your word groups sentences? Rewrite your summary.

_____
_____
_____
_____
_____

Proofread

Read your summary again. Do you see any capitalization errors? Are all of the words spelled correctly? Did you use the correct punctuation and grammar? Use proofreading marks to correct the sentences.

- ❏ Capitalization mistakes
- ❏ Grammar mistakes
- ❏ Punctuation mistakes
- ❏ Spelling mistakes

Publish

Write your final copy on a computer or on the lines below.
MAKE SURE it turns out
- NEAT—Make sure there are no wrinkles, creases, or holes.
- CLEAN—Erase any smudges or dirty spots.
- EASY TO READ—Use your best handwriting and good spacing between words.

_____

_____

_____

_____

_____

_____

_____

_____

_____

_____

_____

_____

_____

_____

3.W.3, 3.W.4, 3.W.5, 3.W.6, 3.W.10, 3.L.1, 3.L.2

Pete ran into the kitchen to get a drink of water. He spied his jar of marbles sitting open on the kitchen table. Pete slipped on some water spilled on the floor. Pete's arm crashed into the table and upset the marble jar.

1. What is the root word of the word **spied**? _____

2. What other word could you use instead of **spied**? _____

3. What action started the accident? _____

4. Predict what will happen next. _____

Day 1

Zoe's class has a math assignment of 25 problems. Their teacher said the assignment must be finished before each student can go out to recess. Zoe went to the restroom and then talked to her friend. She had only finished the first five problems when the bell rang.

1. Write the compound word in this paragraph. _____

2. What is the assignment? _____

3. Did Zoe use her time well? Explain. _____

4. Predict what will happen next. _____

Day 2

Jenny fell on her driveway when her in-line skates hit a stone. Her right knee is cut, and blood is dripping down her leg. "Mom!" she calls. Jenny's mother comes out of the house and runs to her. "Oh, honey, let's go into the house and take care of that."

1. Write the compound word in this paragraph. _____

2. In the passage, what word could replace **cut**: **chopped** or **scraped**? _____

3. If you were reading aloud, would you read "Mom!" loudly or quietly?

   _____

4. Predict what will happen next. _____

Day 3

Evan loves to read books about insects. His class is in the library. He looks in the area where the insect books are usually found. None are there. One of the classes has checked out all of the insect books for reports. He walks to the librarian.

1. Circle the words that can be used instead of **usually**.

   normally   commonly   strangely

2. Why are there no books about insects in the library? _____

3. How do you think Evan feels when he discovers all of the insect books are missing: **frustrated** or **uncaring**? _____

4. Predict what will happen next. _____

Day 4

Deadly Sands

Stories of people and animals sinking into quicksand have been told for hundreds of years. Although some of the stories may be true, it helps to understand what quicksand really is.

Quicksand is a deep bed of light, loose sand that is full of water. On the surface, it looks much like regular sand, but it is really very different. Regular sand is packed firmly and can be walked on. Because quicksand is loose and full of water, it cannot support much weight.

Quicksand usually develops around rivers and lakes. Water collects in the sand and does not drain away. It continues to collect until the sand becomes soft.

Although some objects can float in quicksand, it cannot support the heavy weight of an animal or a person.

1. From the title, can you predict what this passage will be about? Explain.

    _____

2. Find a compound word that is used over four times in the passage. _____

3. Underline the sentence that tells you what quicksand is.

4. Do regular sand and quicksand look similar? Explain. _____

    _____

5. Predict which objects would float in quicksand and which would sink. Circle your predictions.

    A. bicycle   sink   float

    B. cow   sink   float

    C. your lunch   sink   float

    D. shoe   sink   float

    E. mouse   sink   float

3.RL.1, 3.RL.2, 3.RL.3, 3.RL.4, 3.RL.5, 3.RL.6, 3.RL.9, 3.RL.10, 3.RF.3, 3.RF.4, 3.L.3, 3.L.4, 3.L.5, 3.L.6   CD-104598 • © Carson-Dellosa

Name_____

Rewrite the proper nouns with the correct capital letters.
1.   I was born in new york city. _____

Circle the **S** if the words form a complete sentence. Circle the **F** if the words form a fragment.
2.   The zoo is a fun place to go!   **S   F**

Put the correct mark **(. ! ?)** at the end of the sentence.

3.   Sabena at the crunchy apple _____

4.   Underline the word that is incorrect in question 3. Rewrite the word with the correct spelling above it.

Rewrite the proper nouns with the correct capital letters.
1.   We live in orange county. _____

Circle the **S** if the words form a complete sentence. Circle the **F** if the words form a fragment.
2.   I love to see the snakes at the zoo.   **S   F**

Put the correct mark **(. ! ?)** at the end of the sentence.

3.   The clown gave Tripp a candy can _____

4.   Underline the word that is incorrect in question 3. Rewrite the word with the correct spelling above it.

Rewrite the proper nouns with the correct capital letters.
1.   lake superior is the largest lake in the united states. _____

Circle the **S** if the words form a complete sentence. Circle the **F** if the words form a fragment.
2.   Into the alligator's pond.   **S   F**

Put the correct mark **(. ! ?)** at the end of the sentence.

3.   I want to fly my kit _____ .

4.   Underline the word that is incorrect in question 3. Rewrite the word with the correct spelling above it.

Rewrite the proper nouns with the correct capital letters.
1.   chloe spent her summer at camp willow. _____

Circle the **S** if the words form a complete sentence. Circle the **F** if the words form a fragment.
2.   Will you carry the popcorn?   **S   F**

Put the correct mark **(. ! ?)** at the end of the sentence.

3.   Did Jared take car of his puppy _____

4.   Underline the word that is incorrect in question 3. Rewrite the word with the correct spelling above it.

Rewrite the proper nouns with the correct capital letters.

1. When tad went to chicago, he swam in lake michigan.

   _____

2. bermuda is in the atlantic ocean.

   _____

3. The capital of michigan is lansing.

   _____

Circle the **S** if the words form a complete sentence. Circle the **F** if the words form a fragment.

4. The tall zookeeper.   **S   F**
5. The lions are sleeping in the sun.   **S   F**
6. That seal splashed me!   **S   F**

Put the correct mark (**. ! ?**) at the end of each sentence.

7. Wow, it is just what I wanted

8. It is so cold

Underline the words that are incorrect. Then, rewrite the sentences with the correct spellings.

9. Rip peaches are good to eat. _____

   _____

10. Mom wrote a not to my teacher. _____

    _____

3.L.1, 3.L.2

Name_____

Laura Ingalls Wilder wrote eight books about her life growing up in Wisconsin, Kansas, Minnesota, and South Dakota in the 1800s. During her life, she and her family faced many hardships.

1. Who is this passage about? _____

2. What is Laura Ingalls Wilder known for? _____

3. What word in this paragraph is a synonym for the word **problems**?

_____

4. What hardships do you think Laura and her family faced? _____

_____

Day 1

The Ingalls family moved from Kansas to Minnesota and lived in a dugout on the banks of Plum Creek. A dugout is a shelter dug into the side of a hill. The Ingalls lived in this home while they built a new house and a barn.

1. What is a **dugout** as used in this passage? _____

2. How was a dugout a good place to live? _____

3. How was a dugout a difficult place to live? _____

4. Describe the place you live. _____

_____

Day 2

While in Minnesota, Laura's sister Mary became very sick. She ran a high fever. Mary recovered from the sickness, but she had become blind from the high fever. Later, Mary went to a school for the blind. There, she learned Braille and other skills to help her have a better life.

1. What reference book would be more helpful to find the location of Minnesota: an **atlas** or a **dictionary**? _____

2. What caused Laura's sister Mary to become blind? _____

3. How did Mary deal with becoming blind? _____

4. What skills have you learned to help you live a better life? _____

Day 3

Later, Laura and her family moved to South Dakota. They were able to stake claim for land. They built a house on the prairie. Laura and her younger sister went to school in town. Laura would later become a teacher herself.

1. What does it mean to **stake claim**? _____

2. Describe how you imagine Laura and her family moved. _____

_____

3. Describe how you think Laura's school is alike and different from your school.

_____

Day 4

A Frightful Winter

Laura Ingalls Wilder's family was very close. Her parents worked hard to provide a happy family life. But, life on the prairie could be dangerous. One winter, the trains could not get through. Food could not be delivered. The only food they had was some bread. It had to last them the whole winter.

Years after that frightful winter, Laura married Almanzo Wilder. They had a daughter named Rose. Rose later helped her mother write her first book about life on the prairie. This book was called *Little House in the Big Woods*.

1. What things does your family do to stay close? _____

    _____

    _____

2. How was life on the prairie dangerous? _____

    _____

    _____

3. Who helped Laura Ingalls Wilder write her first book? _____

    _____

4. Would you enjoy reading books about life on the prairie? Explain. _____

    _____

    _____

    _____

3.RL.1, 3.RL.2, 3.RL.3, 3.RL.4, 3.RL.5, 3.RL.6, 3.RL.9, 3.RL.10, 3.RF.3, 3.RF.4, 3.L.3, 3.L.4, 3.L.5, 3.L.6

Day 1

Correct the capitalization errors.
1. sally is a babysitter.

Circle the correct verb tense.
2. Carrie (walks, walked) to school yesterday.

Add commas where they are needed.
3. David John and Leo went to the beach.

Change the singular nouns to plural nouns.
4. library _____   city _____

Day 2

Correct the capitalization errors.
1. she is going to babysit for aunt irene on monday.

Circle the correct verb tense.
2. Nick (runs, ran) three miles four days a week.

Add commas where they are needed.
3. Oh what did they do?

Change the singular nouns to plural nouns.
4. grocery _____   firefly _____

Day 3

Correct the capitalization errors.
1. bill and corrina are looking forward to blair's visit.

Circle the correct word.
2. Everyone (accept, except) Carter went to the library.

Add commas where they are needed.
3. They swam ate lunch and played volleyball.

Change the singular nouns to plural nouns.
4. boy _____   country _____

Day 4

Correct the capitalization errors.
1. aunt irene moved to culver city, california, in april.

Circle the correct word.
2. Alfonso (sets, sits) in the front seat with his father.

Add commas where they are needed.
3. Well what did they do with the surfboard?

Change the singular nouns to plural nouns.
4. penny _____   army _____

Correct the capitalization errors.

1. to get to her aunt's home, mackenzie takes the bus.

2. she takes the bus from orange city every tuesday and friday.

3. mackenzie plays with nina and paul all day.

Circle the correct words.

4. "I hope this game is (well, good)," said Father.

5. They drove (to, two, too) the football stadium.

6. "Do you (accept, except) my apology?" asked Austin.

Add commas where they are needed.

7. Andrew Clarke and Vince took turns using the board.

8. The boys took turns floating paddling and riding the waves on the board.

Change the singular nouns to plural nouns.

9. monkey _____

10. pony _____

11. party _____

12. tray _____

Giants of the Forest

Can you imagine a tree as tall as a football field is long? Can you imagine many of them standing together so tall that you cannot see their tops? If you can, then you can imagine a redwood forest.

1. What clues does the title give you about the subject of the passage? _____

2. Does the opening sentence support or contradict your guess? _____

3. What is the subject of this passage? _____

4. This passage compares a redwood tree to a _____.

Day 1

Redwoods are the tallest trees. In fact, they are the tallest living things in the world. The tallest redwood is taller than a 20-story building. It is so big around that six people holding hands can barely reach around it.

1. What two things are compared in this paragraph? _____

2. How are the two things alike? _____
   _____

3. How are the two things different? _____
   _____

4. Estimate how big around a redwood tree is. _____

Day 2

Redwoods are very tough trees. They have a rough, reddish bark that can grow up to one foot thick. The tannin in this special bark helps the trees resist fire, insects, and disease. Many old redwoods have survived terrible storms, floods, and fires.

1. What is the main idea of this paragraph? _____

2. The first detail supports the main idea by telling how _____ the bark is.

3. The second detail supports the main idea by telling three things the bark resists:
   _____   _____   _____

4. The third detail supports the main idea by telling three things old redwoods have survived: _____   _____   _____

Day 3

It is a good thing redwoods are so healthy, for they take many years to grow. They often keep growing for 600 to 1,200 years. A few have even lived for more than 2,000 years! That makes them some of the oldest living things in the world.

1. What is the main idea of this paragraph? _____

2. List one detail that supports the main idea. _____

3. About how long do people live? _____

4. Name one way you are like a redwood tree and one way you are different.
   _____

Day 4

How Redwoods Become Giants

How do redwoods get so big? First, they live where the weather is just right for them. Coast redwood trees grow near the Pacific Ocean in the states of California and Oregon. They live in an area with hot, dry summers and warm, rainy winters. That means they do not have to survive in the cold. Though they do not get much rain, the trees regularly get water from fog.

Another reason redwoods get so big is their resistance to insects and disease. Tannic acid in the thick bark and wood keeps pests from hurting the trees. It also protects redwoods against diseases that infect and kill other kinds of trees.

Even fire has a hard time hurting redwood trees. Old redwoods have ways to guard against forest fires. First, their bark must get very hot in order to burn. Next, they contain a lot of water and burn very slowly. Finally, the needles and branches, which burn more easily than the bark, are far up from the ground. Fire almost never reaches them. In fact, fire helps old redwood forests by clearing out other types of trees from the forest floor.

1. Read the title. What does the title suggest you will read in this passage?

   A. a list of ways people can use redwood trees

   B. types of animals that live in redwood forests

   C. reasons why redwoods live long and grow tall

2. What is the main idea of paragraph 1? _____

3. Which of the following is not a supporting detail for the main idea of paragraph 1?

   A. Redwoods grow near the Pacific Ocean in California and Oregon.

   B. Redwoods live in an area where they are not in danger of freezing.

   C. Redwoods do not get enough water because they do not get much rain.

   D. Redwoods get water from fog.

4. Why do redwoods have better protection than other trees against disease?_____
   _____

5. Explain how redwoods have protection against fire. _____
   _____

6. Which of the following is not a detail that tells how redwoods become giants?

   A. Redwoods live in weather that is right for them.

   B. Redwood bark contains tannic acid, so it resists insects and disease.

   C. Redwoods do not get a lot of water.

   D. Redwoods have special protection against forest fires.

Prewrite/Brainstorm

A paragraph that explains how things are different or the same is called a compare-and-contrast paragraph. Look at the Venn diagram. Three ideas comparing and contrasting snakes and dogs are already shown. Make your own Venn diagram and write more ideas that show how dogs and snakes are the same and different.

snake

snake and dog

dog

eats as needed

both can be pets

needs training

Day 1

Draft

Use the information you wrote about dogs and snakes to write a paragraph comparing and contrasting the two pets. Remember to include a topic sentence and a concluding sentence.

_____

_____

_____

_____

Day 2

Revise

Read your paragraph to a friend. Does it begin with a topic sentence? Do the supporting sentences explain how dogs and snakes are the same? Do they explain how dogs and snakes are different? Did you remember to end with a concluding sentence? Rewrite your paragraph.

_____

_____

_____

_____

Day 3

Proofread

Read your paragraph again. Do you see any capitalization errors? Are all of the words spelled correctly? Did you use the correct punctuation and grammar? Use proofreading marks to correct the sentences.

- ❑ Capitalization mistakes
- ❑ Grammar mistakes
- ❑ Punctuation mistakes
- ❑ Spelling mistakes

Day 4

Publish

Write your final copy on a computer or on the lines below.
MAKE SURE it turns out

- NEAT—Make sure there are no wrinkles, creases, or holes.
- CLEAN—Erase any smudges or dirty spots.
- EASY TO READ—Use your best handwriting and good spacing between words.

_____

_____

_____

_____

_____

_____

_____

_____

_____

_____

_____

_____

3.W.2, 3.W.4, 3.W.5, 3.W.6, 3.L.1, 3.L.2   CD-104598 • © Carson-Dellosa

The Big Bird with the Big Bill

"A wonderful bird is a pelican; her bill will hold more than its belly can." This is true. A pelican has a big pouch under her bill. The pouch will hold more than 3 gallons (11.36 L) of water, far more than a pelican can hold in its stomach.

1. What is the subject of this passage? _____

2. What word in this paragraph means "a pocket that can hold things"? _____

3. What rhyme is quoted in this paragraph? Underline it.

4. Which is bigger—a pelican's bill or its belly? _____

Day 1

North America is home for two varieties of pelicans. The white pelican lives around lakes in the western United States. The brown pelican lives near the ocean in California and around the Gulf of Mexico.

1. What is the difference between North America and the United States? _____
   _____

2. What is another word for **varieties**: **types** or **ages**? _____

3. What two animals does this paragraph compare? _____

4. How are these two kinds of pelicans different? _____
   _____

Day 2

For a while, it seemed that only one kind of pelican might be left. Almost all of the brown pelicans died because of dirty, unsafe water in the Gulf of Mexico. But, people began to clean up the water in time, and now the number of brown pelicans is growing again.

1. What is the problem stated in this paragraph? _____

2. What is the opposite of **unsafe**? _____

3. Is Gulf of Mexico water cleaner or dirtier than it used to be? _____

4. Which type of pelicans almost died out due to dirty water?

   A. brown pelicans   B. white pelicans   C. both   D. neither

Day 3

Both white and brown pelicans are sizable birds. White pelicans weigh about 20 pounds (9.07 kg) and are about 5 feet (1.52 m) long. Brown pelicans are smaller. They weigh only half as much as white pelicans and are a little shorter. Both pelicans eat fish. But, they do not fish in the same way.

1. What word could you use instead of **sizeable**? _____

2. List two ways brown and white pelicans are alike. _____

3. List two ways brown and white pelicans are different. _____

4. Do you agree that pelicans are wonderful birds? Explain. _____
   _____

Day 4

The Big Bird with the Big Bill (continued)

Brown pelicans like to fish alone. They fly over the water looking for fish far below. When they see fish, they dive into the water and scoop them up. They put the fish into their bills like you might put food in a shopping bag. White pelicans like to fish together. They also fly high above the water looking for fish. But, when white pelicans find a group of fish, they land on the water. Then, they form a half circle and start beating their wings on the water. The startled fish swim to the middle of the circle, and the pelicans start their tasty meal.

1. What is the main idea of this paragraph? _____

2. What word in the paragraph means **surprised**? _____

3. What does the author compare a pelican's bill with? _____

4. List one similarity in the way brown and white pelicans fish. _____
    _____

5. List two differences in the way brown and white pelicans fish. _____
    _____
    _____

6. In the space below, draw a picture of a pelican.

Prewrite/Brainstorm

A topic sentence tells the main idea in a paragraph. Supporting sentences explain more about the main idea. Read the topic sentence below. Think about things that support this main idea. Write three things that support the topic sentence.

Friendship is the greatest thing in the world.

_____   _____   _____

Day 1

Draft

Write a paragraph. Use the topic sentence about friendship as your first sentence. Write three sentences that support the main idea.

_____

_____

_____

_____

Day 2

Revise

Read your paragraph to an adult to see how you can make it better. Do you have one main idea? Do your sentences support your main idea? Are the words in the right order? Are your word groups sentences? Rewrite your paragraph.

_____

_____

_____

_____

Day 3

Proofread

Read your paragraph again. Do you see any capitalization errors? Are all of the words spelled correctly? Did you use the correct punctuation and grammar? Use proofreading marks to correct the sentences.

☐   Capitalization mistakes
☐   Grammar mistakes
☐   Punctuation mistakes
☐   Spelling mistakes

Day 4

Publish

Write your final copy on a computer or on the lines below.

MAKE SURE it turns out

- NEAT—Make sure there are no wrinkles, creases, or holes.
- CLEAN—Erase any smudges or dirty spots.
- EASY TO READ—Use your best handwriting and good spacing between words.

_____

_____

_____

_____

_____

_____

_____

_____

_____

_____

_____

_____

_____

3.W.1, 3.W.4, 3.W.5, 3.W.6, 3.W.10, 3.L.1, 3.L.2, 3.L.3

Sunken Treasure

Have you ever read stories about sunken treasure buried at the bottom of the ocean? Maybe you have thought how exciting it would be to look for buried gold. But, you may say, people find treasure only in storybooks.

1. What does the title tell you this passage will be about? _____

2. From the title, does the author seem excited or angry? _____

3. What is the main idea of this paragraph? _____

4. Do you believe you could find buried treasure? _____ Where? _____

Day 1

Kip Wagner from Florida knows treasure is not just in storybooks. He has found eight sunken ships loaded with gold and silver. It all started one day in 1948 when Kip was walking along the beach. He saw something shiny in the sand and stopped to pick it up. To his surprise, it was a "piece of eight," an old Spanish coin of pure gold.

1. Who is this passage about? _____

2. How many years ago was the "piece of eight" found? _____

3. What is the main idea of this paragraph? _____

4. What did Kip find first? _____

Day 2

Many other people would have taken the coin and gone about their business. But, Kip was interested in where the coin came from and what it was worth. He looked at old maps and read history books until he found information about the coin.

1. Circle words that describe Kip's character: determined   curious   lazy

2. What was Kip curious about? _____

3. What would you do if you found a gold coin? _____

    _____

4. What is the main idea of this paragraph? _____

Day 3

Kip found out that in the year 1715, a fleet of 11 Spanish ships had been carrying gold, silver, and jewels from South America to Spain. During a storm, the ships sank. "Perhaps," thought Kip, "the ships and their treasure are still at the bottom of the ocean."

1. What is the main idea of this paragraph? _____

2. Which detail about the ships is **not** in this paragraph?
    A. They carried gold and silver.   B. They sank in a storm.
    C. They sank near Florida.

3. What do you think Kip might do? _____

4. Would you like to look for sunken treasure? Explain. _____

Day 4

Sunken Treasure (continued)

Kip Wagner decided to go on a real-life treasure hunt. First, he flew an airplane over the ocean. He looked near the beach where he found the gold coin.

Soon, he spotted a big dark shape under the water. He marked the spot on a map and made plans to go there by boat. Later, he and some friends dove near the shape. There, at the bottom of the sea, they found cannons from a sunken treasure ship!

Over time, Kip's diving team found jewels from South America. They also found many gold and silver pieces. They had truly found sunken treasure!

1. Would you describe Kip as **adventurous** or **fearful**? Explain.

   _____

   _____

2. What did Kip do first?

   A. find cannons

   B. mark the spot on the map

   C. fly an airplane over the ocean

3. What is the main idea of the entire passage?

   A. Kip Wagner went on a real-life treasure hunt and found sunken treasure.

   B. Kip mapped a dark shape and then went diving to check it out.

4. Circle all of the details that support the main idea in this passage.

   A. From up in an airplane, Kip saw a dark shape under the water.

   B. Kip was lowered from the airplane into the water near the shape.

   C. Kip later returned by boat to the dark shape and dove to check it out.

   D. After several dives, Kip's team found jewels, gold, and silver.

   E. Kip's team found a cannon on the beach.

Prewrite/Brainstorm

Think about ways that schools could recycle. Is recycling a good idea? Is it easy? Write your main idea in the oval. Then, write three ways that schools could recycle.

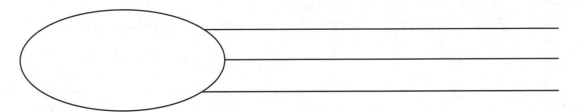

Draft

Write a paragraph about ways that schools could recycle. Use your main idea as the topic sentence. Use your three ideas to write three sentences that support the main idea.

_____

_____

_____

_____

Revise

Read your paragraph and think about how you can make it better. Do you have one main idea? Do your sentences support your main idea? Are the words in the right order? Are your word groups sentences? Rewrite your paragraph.

_____

_____

_____

_____

Proofread

Read your paragraph again. Do you see any capitalization errors? Are all of the words spelled correctly? Did you use the correct punctuation and grammar? Use proofreading marks to correct the sentences.

- ❑ Capitalization mistakes
- ❑ Grammar mistakes
- ❑ Punctuation mistakes
- ❑ Spelling mistakes

Day 1

Day 2

Day 3

Day 4

Publish

Write your final copy on a computer or on the lines below.
MAKE SURE it turns out

- NEAT—Make sure there are no wrinkles, creases, or holes.
- CLEAN—Erase any smudges or dirty spots.
- EASY TO READ—Use your best handwriting and good spacing between words.

_____

_____

_____

_____

_____

_____

_____

_____

_____

_____

_____

_____

_____

_____

3.W.2, 3.W.4, 3.W.5, 3.W.6, 3.W.10, 3.L.1, 3.L.2, 3.L.3

The Lost Ring

Sadie Space Officer was flying on her nightly patrol. She flew close to Mars. Tears rolled down Mars's craters and made huge pools. "What's the matter, Mars?" she asked. "How can I help?"

1. Which word does **craters** rhyme with: **skaters** or **waters**? _____

2. What is someone doing when they are "producing tears"? _____

3. Where does Sadie patrol? _____

4. What does Sadie do when she notices that Mars is upset? _____

Day 1

"One of my moons got a nice ring for a gift. But, the ring is lost. My moon is so sad. Now, it doesn't give any moonlight. My poor moon!" Mars sniffled.

1. What word with a **soft c** is in this paragraph? _____

2. What is **moonlight**? _____

3. Why is Mars's moon sad? _____

4. Why does that make Mars upset? _____

_____

Day 2

"I have an idea!" cried Sadie Space Officer. She raced off toward Saturn. She flew back carrying a sparkling ring. "Will this help?" she asked.

1. Find the word that has an **s** and a **soft c** that sounds like an **s**. _____

2. Does **raced off** tell you that Sadie flew **quickly** or **slowly**? _____

3. Does **sparkling** tell you that the ring is **dull** or **bright**? _____

4. What two things does Sadie do in this paragraph? _____

_____

Day 3

Mars smiled a smile that crossed all of Mars's craters. Sadie tossed the ring to Mars's moon. Instantly, the moon grew bright.

1. Which two words in this paragraph start with a **hard c**? _____

2. What other word could you write instead of **tossed**? _____

3. Was Sadie's solution a good one? Explain. _____

_____

4. Is this story fiction or nonfiction? Explain. _____

_____

Day 4

Mars

Alicia's class was studying the solar system. They learned about many different planets, stars, and moons. Then, they each got to choose one planet or star to write a report about. Alicia wanted to do her report on Jupiter, but that planet was already taken. "Then, I will do my report on Mars because I love its red color," said Alicia.

"Mars is a beautiful color," said her teacher. "In fact, it is often called the Red Planet because it looks like a red star in the night sky." Alicia wrote down this first fact about Mars.

Next, Alicia checked out a book about Mars from the library. She found out that Mars is the fourth planet from the sun. It is only half the size of Earth. But, because it has no oceans or lakes, it has as much land as Earth. There is no rainfall on Mars. The planet has many large deserts with huge dust storms that cover the entire planet. It also has two small moons. Alicia wrote all of these facts in her notebook.

Finally, Alicia looked on the Internet. She found a website that showed robot spacecraft that have landed on Mars. These spacecraft have sent back thousands of pictures. The pictures showed volcanoes, canyons, and channels on Mars. Alicia added more facts and some pictures to her notebook. Then, she used what she had found to make an interesting poster.

"Well done!" said her teacher. "You are now this class's Red Planet expert!"

1. Compare this passage to "The Lost Ring." How are they alike? How are they different?

    _____

    _____

2. In the phrase, "huge dust storms that cover the **entire** planet," what word could you use instead of **entire**? _____

3. How did Alicia solve her problem about not getting to do her report on Jupiter? _____

    _____

4. Put the sentences in order. Write the number in front of each one.

    _____ Alicia looks on the Internet and finds pictures of Mars.

    _____ Alicia's teacher tells her Mars is called the Red Planet.

    _____ Alicia learns that Mars is the fourth planet from the sun.

5. Why does Alicia's teacher call her the class's Red Planet expert at the end of the story instead of at the beginning? _____

 3.RL.1, 3.RL.2, 3.RL.3, 3.RL.4, 3.RL.5, 3.RL.9, 3.RL.10, 3.RI.1, 3.RI.2, 3.RI.3, 3.RI.4, 3.RI.5, 3.RI.8, 3.RI.9, 3.RI.10, 3.RF.3, 3.RF.4, 3.L.4, 3.L.5, 3.L.6   CD-104598 • © Carson-Dellosa

Name_____

Prewrite/Brainstorm

A descriptive paragraph paints a picture in the reader's mind. It describes something. Use the idea web to describe the pet you want.

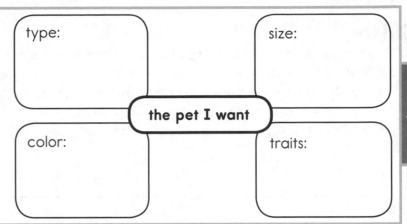

type:

size:

the pet I want

color:

traits:

Draft

Now, use the ideas in the web to write a paragraph describing the pet you want. Remember that the main idea is in the topic sentence.

_____

_____

_____

_____

Revise

Read the paragraph you wrote yesterday. Does it begin with a topic sentence? Do the supporting sentences describe the pet? Did you remember to end with a concluding sentence? Rewrite your paragraph.

_____

_____

_____

_____

Proofread

Read your paragraph again. Do you see any capitalization errors? Are all of the words spelled correctly? Did you use the correct punctuation and grammar? Use proofreading marks to correct the sentences.

- ❑ Capitalization mistakes
- ❑ Grammar mistakes
- ❑ Punctuation mistakes
- ❑ Spelling mistakes

Publish

Write your final copy on a computer or on the lines below.
MAKE SURE it turns out
- NEAT—Make sure there are no wrinkles, creases, or holes.
- CLEAN—Erase any smudges or dirty spots.
- EASY TO READ—Use your best handwriting and good spacing between words.

_____

_____

_____

_____

_____

_____

_____

_____

_____

_____

_____

_____

_____

3.W.2, 3.W.4, 3.W.5, 3.W.6, 3.W.10, 3.L.1, 3.L.2, 3.L.3 CD-104598 • © Carson-Dellosa

A Gift from the Trees

Nothing tastes quite as good on pancakes or waffles as maple syrup. The native people in eastern Canada made maple syrup a long time ago. Native people from the northern part of the United States made it too.

1. Which word has a **hard g** sound and rhymes with **wood**? _____

2. What other word for **good** could be used in this sentence? _____

3. Circle the sentence in this paragraph that is an opinion.

4. Underline the two sentences in this paragraph that are facts.

Day 1

When the settlers came, they learned how to make syrup. Making maple syrup takes a long time, so people who make syrup begin work before the winter snow melts.

1. What word could you write instead of **settlers**?   A. colonists   B. native people

2. Why do syrup makers begin work before the snow melts? _____

_____

3. How did the settlers learn to make syrup? _____

4. Is your answer to question 3 stated or implied? _____

Day 2

Maple syrup comes from the sap of maple trees. Just before spring comes, the trees send sugar and water up from their roots to their branches. This sugar and water mixture is the sap.

1. Does **roots** rhyme with **boots** or **boats**? _____

2. What is **sap**? _____

3. Underline the sentences in this paragraph that are facts.

4. Write an opinion sentence about maple syrup. _____

_____

Day 3

Maple trees of all ages will give sap, but only older trees with big trunks can give sap for syrup without being harmed. Sugar maples and black maples have the best sap for syrup.

1. Circle the word that has a **soft g** sound: ages   give   big   sugar

2. What other word could you write instead of **harmed**? _____

3. What types of trees have the best sap for syrup? _____

4. Are the sentences in this paragraph facts or opinions? _____

Day 4

A Gift from the Trees (continued)

When syrup makers find just the right tree, they hammer a tube called a **spout** into the tree trunk. Then, they hang a bucket under the spout. The sap drips out through the spout and falls into the bucket. When the bucket is full, the syrup makers pour the sap into a big pot. Then, the cooking begins. The pot of sap boils all day on a stove, and, once in a while, people stir the sap as it boils. The smell of maple syrup floats outside and makes people hungry. It smells so good! Boiling makes the water in the sap evaporate, and the sap gets thick and goopy. When it gets thick enough, the sap becomes maple syrup.

It takes a great deal of sap to make syrup. One maple tree gives 15 to 20 gallons (56.78 to 75.7 L) of sap. All of this sap makes only 2 quarts (1.89 L) of syrup. People who make syrup must own many trees and work hard. But, the taste of maple syrup in the morning makes all of the work worthwhile!

1. What is a **spout**? _____

2. Using information from the passage, draw a picture of a spout and bucket collecting sap on the illustration of the maple tree above.

3. Circle one opinion sentence in each paragraph.

4. Underline one fact sentence in each paragraph.

5. This passage states that syrup is a gift from trees. What other gifts come from trees?

_____

3.RI.1, 3.RI.2, 3.RI.3, 3.RI.4, 3.RI.6, 3.RI.7, 3.RI.8, 3.RI.10, 3.RF.3, 3.RF.4, 3.L.3, 3.L.4, 3.L.5, 3.L.6

Prewrite/Brainstorm

An informative paragraph gives information. Use the word web to write information about your family. Write **my family** in the big circle. Write your ideas about your family in the smaller circles. (Use your own paper or a bigger copy of this word web.)

Draft

Write an informative paragraph about your family. Start with the topic sentence **My family is special**. Use your ideas from the word web. Write three supporting sentences and a concluding sentence.

_____
_____
_____
_____

Revise

Read the paragraph you wrote about your family. Does it start with the topic sentence? Does it have at least three supporting sentences? Does it have a concluding sentence that tells the main idea in a different way? Rewrite your paragraph. Use words that are specific.

_____
_____
_____
_____

Proofread

Read your paragraph again. Do you see any capitalization errors? Are all of the words spelled correctly? Did you use the correct punctuation and grammar? Use proofreading marks to correct the sentences.

❐ Capitalization mistakes
❐ Grammar mistakes
❐ Punctuation mistakes
❐ Spelling mistakes

Publish

Write your final copy on a computer or on the lines below.
MAKE SURE it turns out

- NEAT—Make sure there are no wrinkles, creases, or holes.
- CLEAN—Erase any smudges or dirty spots.
- EASY TO READ—Use your best handwriting and good spacing between words.

_____

_____

_____

_____

_____

_____

_____

_____

_____

_____

_____

_____

_____

Name_____

A Turtle Speaks Out

I'm speaking from my home in the Atlantic Ocean off the east coast of the United States. I'm a leatherback turtle, and I'm on the threatened species list along with my friends the green and hawksbill turtles. That scares me! It's tough being a sea turtle!

1. Does the **ough** in **tough** sound like the **ough** in **dough** or in **rough**? _____

2. What is the opposite of **threatened**: **safe** or **endangered**? _____

3. What is the turtle's problem? _____

4. Is this a fiction or nonfiction story? _____ How can you tell? _____
    _____

Day 1

The activities of humans are making life hard for me and my other sea turtle friends. Did you know that we're hunted for our shells? People make ornaments and jewelry from our beautiful shells. And, many people eat turtle meat and eggs!

1. Are the sentences fact or opinion? _____

2. Why does the author use a fictitious character to provide important information? _____

3. Do turtles have good reasons to be scared of humans? Explain. _____
    _____

4. How do turtles act when they see people? _____

Day 2

Life is rough in other ways. You see, female sea turtles lay their eggs on sandy beaches, and baby turtles must run unprotected back to the sea. Many beach areas are populated now. That means people live there, spoiling our natural habitat.

1. Does the **ough** in **rough** sound like the **ough** in **dough** or in **enough**? _____

2. What does **populated** mean? _____

3. How are humans a danger to baby sea turtles? _____

4. What could you do to help protect sea turtle habitats? _____
    _____

Day 3

A big problem occurs when people drive across the turtle paths. But, I can't put all of the blame on humans. Predators such as dogs, birds, raccoons, and crabs eat many of our eggs and hatchlings.

1. Which word has three syllables? _____

2. What is the opposite of **predators**: **prey** or **carnivores**? _____

3. What can beach-buggy owners do to protect sea turtles? _____
    _____

4. If there were no people, would sea turtles be safe? Explain. _____
    _____

Day 4

A Turtle Speaks Out (continued)

Let's say that the eggs hatch, and many of the baby sea turtles make it to the shore. Another problem may appear—water pollution. Oil spills and poisonous chemicals can harm us. We also have to avoid the fishing nets that entangle and drown us. It's tough being a turtle!

But, all is not doom and gloom. Some areas ban items made from turtle shells. Other people help us by putting special devices in fishing nets so that we can be released if we get caught. In some places, laws have been passed to keep vehicles off beaches. Oil companies now have to pay heavy fines and are held responsible for cleaning up oil spills.

Well, time for me to return to my swim. I hope to see you again on some clean, quiet beach on the United States eastern coast.

1. What is the opposite of **released**? _____

2. Besides people and animals, name one other threat to sea turtles. _____
    _____

3. Why do you think the author wants to tell people how hard it is to be a sea turtle?
    _____

4. What does the saying **doom and gloom** mean? _____

5. Match the problem on the left to its solution on the right.

Problem	Solution
1. Turtle shells are used for ornaments and jewelry.	A. Special devices in fishing nets allow turtles to be released.
2. People drive across turtle paths.	B. Companies pay fines and have to clean up oil spills.
3. Fishing nets entangle and drown turtles.	C. Some areas ban things made from turtle shells.
4. Oil spills can harm many turtles.	D. Laws keep vehicles off some beaches.

3.RL.1, 3.RL.2, 3.RL.3, 3.RL.4, 3.RL.5, 3.RL.6, 3.RI.1, 3.RI.2, 3.RI.3, 3.RI.4, 3.RI.6, 3.RI.8, 3.RI.9, 3.RI.10, 3.RF.3, 3.RF.4, 3.L.3, 3.L.4, 3.L.5, 3.L.6   CD-104598 • © Carson-Dellosa

Correct the capitalization errors in the title.
1.   *there are rocks in my socks*

Fill in the blank with the correct word.
2.   May I borrow a piece _____ paper? (**of**, **off**)

Put commas, periods, exclamation points, and question marks where they should be in the sentence.
3.   David asked "What is the longest river"

Fill in the blank with the correct word (**their**, **they're**, or **there**).
4.   Nadia and Liv are feeding _____ pets.

Correct the capitalization errors in the title.
1.   *gus was a friendly ghost*

Fill in the blank with the correct word.
2.   Please take your feet _____ the table. (**off**, **of**)

Put commas, periods, exclamation points, and question marks where they should be in the sentence.
3.   "What are you reading" asked Mark

Fill in the blank with the correct word (**their**, **they're**, or **there**).
4.   _____ feeding the ducks, rabbits, and geese first.

Correct the capitalization errors in the title.
1.   *the book of giant stories*

Fill in the blank with the correct word.
2.   Gabe borrowed some money _____ his friend. (**off**, **from**)

Put commas, periods, exclamation points, and question marks where they should be in the sentence.
3.   "According to this book" said Jill "geese fly the highest"

Fill in the blank with the correct word (**their**, **they're**, or **there**).
4.   "Nadia, would you carry this bag of food over _____?" asked Liv.

Correct the capitalization errors in the title.
1.   *the teeny, tiny witch*

Fill in the blank with the correct word.
2.   I should _____ finished my homework first. (**of**, **have**)

Put commas, periods, exclamation points, and question marks where they should be in the sentence.
3.   "Did you know that only two types of mammals lay eggs" asked Holly

Fill in the blank with the correct word (**their**, **they're**, or **there**).
4.   "I will carry it over _____ if you will watch the rabbits."

Correct the capitalization errors in the titles.

1. *exploring the world of fossils*

2. *the world of insects*

3. *yellow rose of texas*

Fill in the blanks with the correct words.

4. Jennifer must _____ been swimming this afternoon. (**of, have**)

5. "Don't jump _____ the roof!" shouted Mr. Taylor. (**off, of**)

6. I got some pencils _____ my sister. (**off, of, from**)

Put commas, periods, exclamation points, and question marks where they should be in the sentences.

7. "Do spiders live in their webs" asked David

8. "Sure" replied Mark

Fill in the blanks with the correct words.

9. "_____ gone!" shouted Nadia. (**their, they're,** or **there**)

10. The girls looked and saw _____ pet rabbits running off behind the bushes. (**their, they're,** or **there**)

An American Champion

Speed skater Bonnie Blair is the only American woman to have won five Olympic gold medals at the Winter Olympics.

1. From the title, what did you think this passage would be about? _____

_____

2. Who is the "American Champion"? _____

3. What do you think speed skating is? _____

4. How does Bonnie Blair differ from other Olympians? _____

Day 1

Born on March 18, 1964, Bonnie was the youngest in a speed-skating family. Her five older brothers and sisters were champion skaters who encouraged her. They put a pair of skates over Bonnie's shoes when she was two years old because of her tiny feet.

1. Describe Bonnie's family. _____

2. Who do you think wanted Bonnie to skate more, her family or Bonnie herself? Explain. _____

3. What has your family encouraged you to learn? _____

4. From family stories, describe what you were like at two years old. _____

_____

Day 2

As Bonnie grew, she trained hard six days a week. Bonnie kept this up until she was the world's best female speed skater. She won her first Olympic gold medal in the 500-meter race in 1988. In 1992, she won both the 500-meter and the 1,000-meter Olympic races in Albertville, France. She won again in 1994 in Lillehammer, Norway.

1. How did Bonnie train to become an Olympic athlete? _____

2. What word in this paragraph is a synonym for **practiced**? _____

3. Name two countries where Bonnie competed in the Olympics. _____

4. Describe a time that you were rewarded for your hard work. _____

_____

Day 3

Bonnie's Olympic successes made her famous all over the world. Bonnie retired from speed skating in 1995 to focus on other competitions.

1. What was the effect of Bonnie's Olympic successes? _____

2. Have you ever heard about Bonnie Blair? _____

3. In what other competitions do you think Bonnie Blair might have competed?

_____

4. Write one question you would like to ask Bonnie Blair. _____

_____

Day 4

Jane of the Jungle

When Jane Goodall decided to study chimpanzees in 1960, her friends told her not to. Jane wanted to study these animals in their wild home. People said her plan was foolish. These chimpanzees lived in Tanzania, Africa!

She would be in danger because chimpanzees are strong enough to harm a person. Or, she might never even get close to the chimps. Then, her trip would be for nothing. But, Jane was not afraid. She packed her notebooks and set off on her trip.

Jane set up her camp in the Gombe Stream Game Reserve near the chimpanzees. When the chimps saw her, they ran away in fear. But, Jane waited patiently, watching the animals through her field glasses.

As Jane got used to Africa, the chimpanzees got used to her. Finally, after many months, the chimps let Jane get close enough to study them without field glasses.

Jane got to know the chimpanzees so well that they came to visit her and became her friends. She gave them names, like "Greybeard" and "Olly." Jane watched them and wrote down what she saw in her notebook. By watching carefully, Jane learned many new things about chimps. She found out that they sometimes eat meat, and that baby chimps love to tease.

In the years Jane Goodall spent with the chimpanzees, she learned many things. She spent time doing what she loved and helped people learn more about chimpanzees. Her "foolish" trip turned out not to be so foolish after all!

1. Who is the passage about? _____

2. Where does this passage take place? _____

3. Was Jane able to get up close to the chimpanzees at first? Explain. _____

   _____

4. In what ways were the chimpanzees Jane studied like people? _____

   _____

5. Why does the author say "her 'foolish' trip turned out not to be so foolish after all"?

   _____

   _____

3.RI.1, 3.RI.2, 3.RI.3, 3.RI.8, 3.RF.3, 3.RF.4   CD-104598 • © Carson-Dellosa

Name_____

Prewrite/Brainstorm

Think of three things you are good at. These things may include sports, hobbies, or skills. In the oval, write the topic sentence **I am good at many things**. Then, on the lines, write three things about the topic. You will use this information to write an introductory paragraph for an essay about what you are good at.

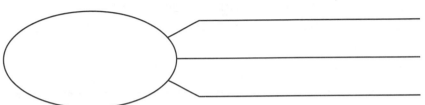

Draft

Write an introductory paragraph about what you are good at. Use the three ideas you wrote in the list.

_____

_____

_____

_____

Revise

Read your paragraph to an adult. Be sure your ideas are complete sentences. Do your ideas support the topic sentence? Change nouns, verbs, and adjectives to more specific words. Rewrite your ideas in a new paragraph.

_____

_____

_____

_____

Proofread

Read your paragraph again. Do you see any capitalization errors? Are all of the words spelled correctly? Did you use the correct punctuation and grammar? Use proofreading marks to correct the sentences.

❏   Capitalization mistakes
❏   Grammar mistakes
❏   Punctuation mistakes
❏   Spelling mistakes

Day 1

Day 2

Day 3

Day 4

Publish

Write your final copy on a computer or on the lines below.
MAKE SURE it turns out

- NEAT—Make sure there are no wrinkles, creases, or holes.
- CLEAN—Erase any smudges or dirty spots.
- EASY TO READ—Use your best handwriting and good spacing between words.

_____

_____

_____

_____

_____

_____

_____

_____

_____

_____

_____

_____

_____

3.W.2, 3.W.4, 3.W.5, 3.W.6, 3.W.10, 3.L.1, 3.L.2, 3.L.3

Vasco de Balboa

Vasco de Balboa was born in Spain in 1475. He heard stories about Columbus discovering America. In 1501, Balboa sailed to Hispaniola, an island near South America. He later traveled to a settlement in Central America called Darien.

1. Whom is this passage about? _____

2. Do you think Balboa grew up speaking English, Spanish, or French? _____

3. How did Balboa travel? _____

4. What effect do you think the stories about Columbus had on Balboa?
   A. They scared him.   B. They made him want to be an explorer.

Day 1

Balboa became a popular governor of Darien. But, in 1513, he left Darien to search for treasures. It was during this trip that Balboa discovered what we now call the Pacific Ocean.

1. Underline the sentence that tells that the people of Darien liked Balboa.

2. What was Balboa's goal when he left Darien? _____

3. What is Balboa most famous for today? _____

4. Would you like to have been an explorer in Balboa's time? Explain. _____

   _____

Day 2

Balboa was excited about his new discovery. But, when he returned to Darien, he found that a new governor named Pedrarias had replaced him. Balboa moved to a different site and built a city. He built new ships for exploration and made many friends.

1. What did Balboa find when he returned from his travels? _____

2. How did Balboa solve the problem of being replaced? _____

3. How did he stay involved in exploration? _____

4. Do you think Balboa was probably a likeable man? Explain. _____

   _____

Day 3

In 1518, Pedrarias accused Balboa of treason. Balboa was innocent, but he was arrested and jailed. Pedrarias sentenced Balboa to death.

1. Who was Pedrarias? (See Day 3.) _____

2. What is **treason**: trying to **work for the government** or trying to **overthrow the government**? _____

3. What is the opposite of **innocent**? _____

4. Was what happened to Balboa at the end of his life **fair** or **unfair**? Explain.

   _____

Day 4

The North Star

The North Star is one of the most famous stars. Its star name is Polaris. It is called the North Star because it shines almost directly over the North Pole. If you are at the North Pole, the North Star is overhead. As you travel farther south, the star seems lower in the sky. Only people in the Northern Hemisphere can see the North Star.

Because the North Star is always in the same spot in the sky, it has been used for years to give direction to people at night. Sailors used the North Star to navigate through the oceans.

Polaris, like all stars, is always moving. Thousands of years from now, another star will get to be the North Star. Vega was the North Star for thousands of years before it moved out of position, and Polaris became the new North Star.

1. What is this passage about? _____

2. The name **Polaris** most likely comes from which name?

   A. polecat

   B. polar bear

   C. North Pole

3. The North Star might be one of the most famous stars because

   A. it is always moving.

   B. it is always in the same spot in the sky.

   C. it is difficult to find in the sky.

4. Another star will someday get to be the North Star because

   A. stars are always moving.

   B. Polaris will burn out.

   C. scientists rename the North Star every 50 years.

5. Do you live in the Northern Hemisphere or the Southern Hemisphere? _____
   _____ How can you tell? _____
   _____

Prewrite/Brainstorm

Now, you are ready to write the second paragraph of your essay about things you are good at. (See Week 32.) Write the three things you chose in the spaces provided. Under each skill, talent, or hobby write a detail or example to describe it.

[ ]   [ ]   [ ]

_____   _____   _____

Draft

Write a paragraph describing the things you are good at. Use transition words such as **one**, **another**, and **last** to connect your ideas.

_____

_____

_____

_____

Revise

Read the paragraph you wrote yesterday to an adult. Be sure your ideas are complete sentences. Change nouns, verbs, and adjectives to more specific words. Rewrite your ideas in a new paragraph.

_____

_____

_____

_____

Proofread

Read your paragraph again. Do you see any capitalization errors? Are all of the words spelled correctly? Did you use the correct punctuation and grammar? Use proofreading marks to correct the sentences.

- ❒   Capitalization mistakes
- ❒   Grammar mistakes
- ❒   Punctuation mistakes
- ❒   Spelling mistakes

Publish

Write your final copy on a computer or on the lines below.
MAKE SURE it turns out

- NEAT—Make sure there are no wrinkles, creases, or holes.
- CLEAN—Erase any smudges or dirty spots.
- EASY TO READ—Use your best handwriting and good spacing between words.

_____

_____

_____

_____

_____

_____

_____

_____

_____

_____

_____

_____

_____

Sound

It is easy to take sound for granted. But, do you really know what sound is? Sound is caused by something quivering back and forth. This shaking motion is called a **vibration**.

1. What sounds do you hear right now? _____

2. What is a **vibration**? _____

3. Is the second sentence of this paragraph a statement or a question? _____

4. All sound is caused by
    A. music and talking.   B. vibrations in the air.   C. airplanes and machines.

Vibrations travel through the air, and you hear them as sounds. You can hear many sounds at the same time because the air can carry many vibrations at one time.

1. How many syllables does **vibrations** have? _____

2. What is another word or phrase for **many**? _____

3. How many sounds can you hear at the same time?
    A. one   B. more than one

4. The air carries many vibrations, which you hear
    A. as wind.   B. one at a time.   C. as sounds.

Different sounds are created according to how fast something vibrates. The faster it vibrates, the higher the sound. A slower vibration causes a lower sound.

1. Which two-syllable words in the last sentence rhyme? _____

2. Write the opposites next to the words.

    faster _____   higher _____

3. Fill in the blanks. Fast vibrations cause _____ sounds. Slow vibrations cause _____ sounds.

4. Different sounds are made according to
    A. how fast something vibrates.   B. how hot the air is.   C. your hearing.

Unpleasant sounds are called noise. Some noise can be harmful to your hearing. Loud noises, such as those from airplanes and machines, can even cause hearing loss. But, other sounds, such as music or talking, are not dangerous—just pleasant.

1. Which three-syllable word has a prefix that means **not**? _____

2. Which two words in this paragraph are opposites? _____

3. Circle the sounds that might be dangerous to your hearing:
    baby giggling   chainsaw   rock music concert   kitten meowing

4. Complete the summary sentence. Sounds can be _____ or _____.

Jackie Robinson

As a young boy, Jackie Robinson started getting in trouble. A neighbor told Jackie that he would upset his mother if she knew what he was doing. The neighbor also told him that he would be showing more bravery if he did not do what his friends wanted him to do. Jackie listened. He decided to become active in sports.

In 1945, professional baseball was still segregated. Jackie played shortstop for the Kansas City Monarchs, a team in the Negro League. It was at this time that the president of the Brooklyn Dodgers, Branch Rickey, recognized Jackie's talent in baseball.

Branch Rickey was determined to make Jackie Robinson the first African American player in Major League Baseball. Jackie started playing with the Brooklyn Dodgers' farm club. Rickey advised Jackie not to fight back when people were unkind to him.

In 1947, Jackie started playing professional baseball for the Brooklyn Dodgers. At first, his teammates did not like playing with him. However, when other teams teased Jackie, his teammates stood up for him. He was selected as Rookie of the Year. In 1949, he was nominated the Most Valuable Player in the National League. In 1955, he helped the Dodgers win the World Series.

Jackie Robinson paved the way for African American men to play in the major leagues. In 1962, he was inducted into the National Baseball Hall of Fame. In 1972, Jackie Robinson died at the age of 53.

1. Does the title give you any clues about who Jackie Robinson is? Explain. _____

_____

2. What important choice did Jackie make as a child? _____

3. What does it mean that baseball was still segregated in 1945? _____

4. What is Jackie Robinson famous for? _____

5. What advice did Branch Rickey give Jackie? _____

_____

6. Do you think this was good advice? Explain. _____

_____

Prewrite/Brainstorm

Write a conclusion paragraph for your essay about things you are good at. (See Week 32 and Week 34.) Your conclusion paragraph should sum up the things you chose to write about. Write the three things you are good at in the graphic organizer.

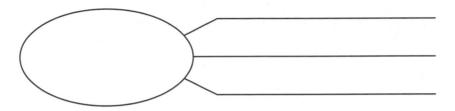

Draft

Write your concluding paragraph. Begin your paragraph with a transition phrase such as **in conclusion**, **finally**, or **to summarize**.

_____

_____

_____

_____

Revise

Read your paragraph to an adult. Be sure your ideas are complete sentences. Change nouns, verbs, and adjectives to more specific words. Rewrite your ideas in a new paragraph.

_____

_____

_____

_____

Proofread

Read your paragraph again. Do you see any capitalization errors? Are all of the words spelled correctly? Did you use the correct punctuation and grammar? Use proofreading marks to correct the sentences.

- ❏ Capitalization mistakes
- ❏ Grammar mistakes
- ❏ Punctuation mistakes
- ❏ Spelling mistakes

Publish

Write your final copy on a computer or on the lines below.
MAKE SURE it turns out

- NEAT—Make sure there are no wrinkles, creases, or holes.
- CLEAN—Erase any smudges or dirty spots.
- EASY TO READ—Use your best handwriting and good spacing between words.

_____

_____

_____

_____

_____

_____

_____

_____

_____

_____

_____

_____

_____

_____

Jose and his grandfather wanted to plant a garden that would attract butterflies. They discovered that because butterflies must eat in the larval stage, a butterfly garden must provide food that caterpillars like. Because butterflies must also eat in the adult stage, a butterfly garden must also provide food that adult butterflies like.

1. Who are the characters in this paragraph? _____

2. What do they want to do? _____

3. Explain the effect. Butterflies must eat in the larval stage, so _____.

4. State the cause. _____, so their garden needs food that adult butterflies like to eat.

Insects kept eating the leaves of Delia's garden plants. Because pesticides can harm the environment, Delia wanted a natural solution. She found out that most ladybugs eat insect pests but do not damage a garden. Ladybugs make perfect plant guards.

1. Who is the character in this paragraph? _____

2. What is her problem? _____

3. Explain the effect. Pesticides can harm the environment, so _____.

4. State the cause. Ladybugs make perfect plant guards because _____

_____.

Thousands of years ago, glaciers—huge masses of slowly moving ice—covered the earth. Temperatures grew colder and glaciers grew larger. Because glaciers pick up parts of land as they move, glaciers can carve out large areas.

1. What is a **glacier**? _____

2. Do glaciers stay in one place? _____

3. Explain the effect. Because temperatures grew colder, _____

_____.

4. State the cause. Because _____, glaciers carve out the earth.

Warming temperatures caused the glaciers to melt. When the glaciers melted, there were huge holes left where the glaciers used to be. Water from melting glaciers and from rain filled these huge holes. They were no longer holes. They were lakes such as Lake Superior, Lake Michigan, Lake Huron, Lake Erie, and Lake Ontario.

1. Name two lakes that were caused by melting glaciers. _____

2. Where did the water that filled the holes come from? _____

3. Explain the effect. Warming temperatures caused _____.

4. State the cause. Great lakes were formed as a result of _____

_____.

Herbs for Healing

Native Americans have used plants as medicines for many years. Herbs and other plants can be used to help cure illnesses. The plants are collected and dried. Then, they are ground into powder. Water is added to make teas to drink and pastes to apply to the skin. Every part of the plants is used: stems, leaves, flowers, bark, and roots.

Garlic cloves have been used for insect stings. Pinesap has been used to heal cuts. Sunflowers can soothe a blister. Witch hazel works on sprains and bruises. A tea made from slippery elm can cure sore throats. Dandelion tea is good for heartburn. Willow bark could be used to cure a headache. Sword fern tea has been used to cure dandruff. Many of these herbs are available in drugstores.

1. What letter is silent in the word **herb**? _____

2. What is a **paste** in the passage? _____

3. What parts of a plant can be used as medicine? _____

_____

4. What was the author's purpose for this passage?

   A. to entertain the reader with interesting facts about Native Americans

   B. to inform the reader about different ways plants can be used as medicine

   C. to persuade the reader to use herbs as medicine

5. Do you use plants to stay healthy? Explain. _____

_____

 3.RI.1, 3.RI.2, 3.RI.3, 3.RI.4, 3.RI.6, 3.RI.8, 3.RI.10, 3.L.2, 3.L.3, 3.L.4, 3.L.5, 3.L.6 CD-104598 • © Carson-Dellosa

Name_____

Prewrite/Brainstorm

Write a report about something you are interested in. Write the topic on the top line. Then, complete the KWL chart on your own paper. Use a book or the Internet to find information that you want to know about your topic.

_____

What I **K**now	What I **W**ant to Learn	What I **L**earned

Draft

Use the information from the KWL chart to write about your topic. Be sure to organize your ideas.

_____
_____
_____
_____

Revise

Read the paragraph you wrote yesterday. Be sure your ideas are sentences. Change nouns, verbs, and adjectives to more specific words. Rewrite your ideas in a new paragraph.

_____
_____
_____
_____

Proofread

Read your paragraph again. Do you see any capitalization errors? Are all of the words spelled correctly? Did you use the correct punctuation and grammar? Use proofreading marks to correct the sentences.

- ❏ Capitalization mistakes
- ❏ Grammar mistakes
- ❏ Punctuation mistakes
- ❏ Spelling mistakes

Publish

Write your final copy on a computer or on the lines below.
MAKE SURE it turns out

- NEAT—Make sure there are no wrinkles, creases, or holes.
- CLEAN—Erase any smudges or dirty spots.
- EASY TO READ—Use your best handwriting and good spacing between words.

_____

_____

_____

_____

_____

_____

_____

_____

_____

_____

_____

_____

_____

3.W.2, 3.W.4, 3.W.5, 3.W.6, 3.W.7, 3.W.8, 3.W.10, 3.L.1, 3.L.2, 3.L.3

Mayan Indians

The ancient Mayan Indians lived in Central America and southern Mexico. Today, descendants of the Mayan people still live there. During the peak of their civilization, they lived in the tropical rain forests of what is now Guatemala.

1. Is the **c** in **central** and **civilizations** a **hard c** or a **soft c**? _____

2. What are **descendants**? _____

3. What is this passage mostly about?   A. where the Maya live   B. rain forests

4. Finish this summary sentence. Modern and ancient Mayan people lived in _____
_____.

Day 1

The Maya developed the first advanced form of writing, called **hieroglyphics**. Records of dates and important events were written on pottery, monuments, and palace walls. The Mayan people lived and wrote until the Spanish invaded during the 16th century.

1. Circle the words with a **long a**: advanced   dates   palace   invaded   overcame

2. What is the opposite of **invaded**: **attacked** or **defended**? _____

3. What is this passage mostly about?   A. Mayan writing   B. Mayan pottery

4. Finish this summary sentence. The Maya developed and used hieroglyphics to
_____.

Day 2

Mayan scholars studied the moon and the planets. They made accurate records and predictions of their cycles. They used what they knew about astronomy to develop two calendars. One calendar predicted good or bad luck. The second calendar had 365 days.

1. What word starts with a **soft c**? _____
   What word starts with a **hard c**? _____

2. What word in this passage is the opposite of **inaccurate**? _____

3. What is this passage mostly about?   A. Mayan calendars   B. Mayan astronomy

4. Finish this summary sentence. Mayan scholars knew a lot about _____
   and used it to _____.

Day 3

Another great Mayan cultural advancement was mathematics. The Maya had a number system that consisted of dots and bars. This number system included a symbol for zero. The Maya were probably the first people to use the idea of "zero" as a number.

1. Which word has the **long a** sound: **great** or **had**? _____

2. What symbol for zero do you use in math? _____

3. What is this passage mostly about?   A. Mayan zeros   B. Mayan mathematics

4. Finish this summary sentence. In Mayan mathematics, there was _____.

Day 4

Mayan Indians (continued)

The Mayan heritage continues with many people of Mexico and Central America. More than 20 languages and dialects are said to be created from the ancient Mayan language. Many of their descendants still practice some of the traditional religious customs. Also, the ruins of ancient Mayan cities are visited each year by many tourists.

1. Underline all of the words in the paragraph that start with a **hard c**. Which one has a **long a**?

   _____

2. What word in this paragraph means the opposite of **new building**? _____

   _____

3. What is this paragraph mostly about?

   A. the Maya today   B. the Mayan religion

4. Circle all of the things you could still find in Mexico and Central America.

   A. languages related to the ancient Mayan language

   B. descendants of the ancient Maya

   C. people practicing some ancient Mayan religious customs

   D. Maya living and speaking exactly like the ancient Maya

   E. old Mayan ruins

   F. tourists creating new Mayan languages

5. Use words from the passage to finish this summary.

   The paragraph is about _____.

   You can still see this heritage in the l_____, r_____

   c_____, and r_____.

Name_____

Prewrite/Brainstorm

Write a narrative about the ancient Mayan culture. Use this section to write facts you learned about the Mayan culture from the reading in Week 39.

_____

_____

_____

_____

_____

Day 1

Draft

Use your list from Day 1 to write a narrative about the Maya. Remember to include a beginning, a middle, and an ending.

_____

_____

_____

_____

_____

Day 2

Revise

Read your narrative aloud to someone else. Does your narrative have a beginning, a middle, and an ending? Can you add details to make your writing more interesting? Rewrite your ideas in a new paragraph.

_____

_____

_____

_____

Day 3

Proofread

Read your paragraph again. Do you see any capitalization errors? Are all of the words spelled correctly? Did you use the correct punctuation and grammar? Use proofreading marks to correct the sentences.

- ❐ Capitalization mistakes
- ❐ Grammar mistakes
- ❐ Punctuation mistakes
- ❐ Spelling mistakes

Day 4

Publish

Write your final copy on a computer or on the lines below.
MAKE SURE it turns out
- NEAT—Make sure there are no wrinkles, creases, or holes.
- CLEAN—Erase any smudges or dirty spots.
- EASY TO READ—Use your best handwriting and good spacing between words.

_____

_____

_____

_____

_____

_____

_____

_____

_____

_____

_____

_____

_____

_____

3.W.3, 3.W.4, 3.W.5, 3.W.6, 3.W.7, 3.W.8, 3.W.10, 3.L.1, 3.L.2, 3.L.3

Answer Key

Page 9
Day 1: 1. blackbirds and a coyote; 2. coyote, because of the title; 3. fiction; 4. Birds do not gather to sing and dance before they head south for the winter. **Day 2:** 1. blackbird; 2. help, Accept any reasonable answer. 3. They liked to have fun. 4. proud, (underlined) I could be the great king of the coyotes. **Day 3:** 1. oo as in boot; 2. the blackbirds' feathers; 3. Answers will vary. 4. Answers will vary. **Day 4:** 1. jabbed; 2. yes, because he wanted to be king of the coyotes; 3. Answers will vary. 4. Answers will vary.

Page 10
1. bruised; 2. wisdom; 3. courage; 4. A; 5. foolish; He realized that the ability to fly would not make him a great king. 6. Answers will vary.

Page 11
Day 1: 1. "A Night in the Desert"; 2. a daisy, an iris; 3. Fleas, flies, and fish are fantastic frog food. 4. mouse, octopus; **Day 2:** 1. "Watch Out!"; 2. a zinnia, a forget-me-not; 3. Pilar picks petunias, peonies, and pansies. 4. man, fungus; **Day 3:** 1. "Rudy's Rowdy Robots"; 2. a lilac, an Indian paintbrush; 3. Does Ivan live in Illinois, Idaho, or Iowa? 4. child, tomato; **Day 4:** 1. "I Am Not a Penguin"; 2. an orange blossom, an apple blossom; 3. Joanna jumps, jogs, and juggles. 4. wolf, hero

Page 12
1. "Cars, Trains, Bikes, and Planes"; 2. "The Worst Day of My Life"; 3. a magnolia blossom, an azalea; 4. a petunia, an impatiens; 5. an orchid, a water lily; 6. Julio is shopping for pens, pencils, and erasers. 7. Mia is taking a trip to Washington, Oregon, and California. 8. John, Dion, and Miguel are going to the skate park. 9. goose, man; 10. brush, shelf

Page 13
Day 1: 1. Southwestern; 2. a Navajo home made of wood and mud; 3. (underlined) Their homes, called hogans, were made of wood and mud and were built in different shapes. 4. They lived in hogans. **Day 2:** 1. brought; 2. never; 3. (underlined) While the shape of the hogans could vary, some characteristics of the houses were always the same. 4. The door always faced east. **Day 3:** 1. mighty;

2. stood for, meant; 3. (underlined) Hogans were constructed with four mighty posts to hold up the roof. 4. Answers will vary but should include information about the meanings of the posts. **Day 4:** 1. clockwise; 2. B; 3. After a house was built, the Navajo blessed the house. 4. Answers will vary but should include information about how the house was blessed.

Page 14
1. fought, fighting, nighttime, night; nighttime; 2. wise; 3. A; 4. C; 5. Bats fly at night because they are not a friend to either birds or animals.

Page 15
Day 1: 1. Alex, Tuesdays, Thursdays; 2. (circled) drinks; 3. trees'; 4. (circled) monkeys; **Day 2:** 1. We, Fourth, July; 2. (circled) bakes; 3. squirrels'; 4. (circled) parties; **Day 3:** 1. Jenna's, Valentine's Day; 2. (circled) drives; 3. dog's; 4. (circled) babies; **Day 4:** 1. Kelly, Ellen's, Friday; 2. (circled) share; 3. children's; 4. (circled) turkeys

Page 16
1. My, May; 2. In, January, Saturday; 3. Jamie's, Hanukkah, December; 4. (circled) wears; 5. (circled) live; 6. Brad's; 7. bird's; 8. dad's; 9. (circled) valleys; 10. (circled) stories

Page 17
Day 1: 1. owls; 2. communicate; 3. mew; 4. howls, noises, and movements; **Day 2:** 1. howl, growl; 2. It is willing to fight. 3. howl, snarl, growl, bark; 4. Answers will vary. **Day 3:** 1. short a; 2. backward; 3. Answers will vary, but should refer to being in charge. 4. head, tail; **Day 4:** 1. playful; 2. A; 3. Answers will vary. 4. It wants to play.

Page 18
1. rain, makes, face; 2. fruit, because it is a plant; 3. Come here; in blossom; Your face on gardens looks; 4. thunder; 5. Thunder is asked to "come here" and "look" and also is described as having a face that looks on gardens.

Page 19
Day 1: 1. "How Much Is That Doggie in the Window?" 2. (circled) will (underlined) sing; 3. My mother grows roses, daisies, and violets in her garden. 4. You're; **Day 2:** 1. *The Biography of Helen Keller*; 2. (circled) will (underlined) teach; 3. no commas needed; 4. your; **Day 3:** 1. *Ranger Rick*; 2. (circled) can (underlined) come; 3. There are maple, pine, oak, and elm trees on my street. 4. You're; **Day 4:** 1. *Green Eggs and Ham*; 2. (circled) Can (underlined) watch; 3. We study spelling, math, history, and art in my class. 4. Your

Page 20
1. "Twinkle, Twinkle, Little Star"; 2. *The Big Book of Lizards*; 3. (circled) will (underlined) write; 4. (circled) can (underlined) fly; 5. (circled) will (underlined) rise; 6. Claire, Philip, Tara, Jose, and I went to the movies together. 7. Tara brought her dogs Peaches, Romeo, and Clyde to the park. 8. Mischa's favorite colors are yellow, purple, blue, and pink. 9. your; 10. You're

Page 21
Day 1: 1. Japan; 2. spring; 3. outside, because trees grow outside; 4. Answers will vary. **Day 2:** 1. to the park; 2. one week; 3. Answers will vary. 4. Answers will vary. **Day 3:** 1. until after dark; 2. at night; 3. Answers will vary. 4. Answers will vary. **Day 4:** 1. Their flowers are gone. 2. same time next year; 3. Answers will vary. 4. Answers will vary.

Page 22
1. lane, window-pane; 2. rattle; 3. He loves it and thinks it is beautiful. He uses words like "beautiful" and "welcome"; 4. Answers will vary. 5. B

Page 23
Day 1: 1. Have; 2. (circled) longest; 3. isn't, is not; shouldn't, should not; 4. women, potatoes; **Day 2:** 1. The, Georgia, O'Keeffe; 2. (circled) loudest; 3. couldn't, could not; aren't, are not; 4. halves, echoes; **Day 3:** 1. Even, Georgia; 2. (circled) colder; 3. wasn't, was not; didn't, did not; 4. shelves, deer; **Day 4:** 1. O'Keeffe, Wisconsin; 2. (circled) larger; 3. don't, do not; weren't, were not; 4. geese, mice

Page 24
1. O'Keeffe, Chicago, York, Texas; 2. She; 3. When, America's; 4. (circled) strongest; 5. (circled) faster; 6. (circled) funniest; 7. can't, cannot; haven't, have not; 8. wouldn't, would not; won't, will not; 9. monkeys, halves; 10. geese, women

Page 25
Day 1: 1. knight in training; 2. letter; 3. the author's father; 4. interesting; **Day 2:** 1. Sir Stephen; 2. Underlining may include: taking care of Sir Stephen's horses; serving him as needed; learning to spar with a sword; learning to hunt with a falcon; playing chess and other games that require skill and strategy; 3. Answers will vary. 4. continuing; He seems happy with what he is learning. **Day 3:** 1. eight; 2. He is excited to become a squire. 3. Answers will vary. 4. Answers will vary. **Day 4:** 1. in a contest called jousting; 2. a long, blunt spear; 3. Answers will vary. 4. interesting; (underlined) most exciting thing squires do

Page 26
1. Arthur; his father; 2. Squire Robert; 3. a metal suit; 4. Drawings will vary but should include a unicorn. 5. Drawings will vary.

Page 27
Day 1: 1. Mr. Oliver Sanchez, Silver Springs Drive, Bangor, Maine; 2. came; 3. "Jill won too medals," announced the coach. 4. (strike through) two; **Day 2:** 1. Mrs. Hannah Chadwick, Pine Street, Garnet, Montana; 2. ate; 3. Todd said, "I like dogs to." 4. (strike through) too; **Day 3:** 1. Shelby Peters, Sunshine Lane, Davies, Florida; 2. saw; 3. "I'm going two walk to school," said Sue. 4. (strike through) to; **Day 4:** 1. Nathan Avery, Tundra Road, Barrow, Alaska; 2. said; 3. "Hit the ball too me!" Brian yelled. 4. (strike through) to

Page 28
1. Casey Walsh, Center Street, Littleton, Maine; 2. Tyrone Hernandez, Wells Avenue, Claremont, California; 3. came; 4. saw; 5. said; 6. (underlined) "I love apple pie," Emma told me. 7. (underlined) "You will like this story," Joey said. 8. correct as is; 9. (strike through) too; 10. (strike through) to

Page 29

Day 1: 1. A; 2. winter; 3. in frozen rivers, lakes, and streams; 4. fishing in winter; **Day 2:** 1. frozen lakes; 2. cold; 3. Answers will vary. 4. Answers will vary. **Day 3:** 1. little houses; 2. (underlined) an ax, fishing lines; 3. Answers will vary. 4. Answers will vary. **Day 4:** 1. a "tip-up"; 2. C; 3. a little flag pop up; 4. Answers will vary.

Page 30

1. Answers will vary. 2. January morning, frozen river behind Jack's house; 3. Jack enjoys spending time with his grandpa. 4. a boot; 5. Answers will vary.

Page 31

Day 1: The brainstorming activity should contain five ideas or words related to the topic. **Day 2:** The first draft should build on ideas taken from the brainstorming activity. **Day 3:** The next draft should show improvements in clarity and cohesiveness. **Day 4:** The final draft should show proofreading marks where needed.

Page 32

The content of writing samples will vary. Check to be sure that students have correctly completed all of the earlier steps in the writing process and have followed the instructions for publishing their work.

Page 33

Day 1: 1. careless; 2. hat; 3. a doll; 4. Her new owner is careless and forgetful. **Day 2:** 1. A; 2. unhappy or sad; 3. He misses fighting fires. 4. at the fire chief's house; **Day 3:** 1. homeless; 2. tangled; 3. He is homeless and needs to find food. 4. He found a house where the owners put out a bowl of tuna every morning. **Day 4:** 1. A; 2. nocturnal; 3. It is hard for Shera to find food. Then, she flies into a window. 4. in a new housing development where there used to be lots of trees

Page 34

1. (circled) sunlight, sightless, bright; sightless; 2. bright; 3A. Joseph; 3B. Abigail; 3C. Kayla; 4. Abigail: morning, autumn; Kayla: evening, summer; Joseph: night, winter; 5. Answers will vary.

Page 35

Day 1: The brainstorming activity should contain various ideas or words related to the Five W's. **Day 2:** The first draft should build on ideas taken from the brainstorming activity. **Day 3:** The next draft should show improvements in clarity and cohesiveness. **Day 4:** The final draft should show proofreading marks where needed.

Page 36

The content of writing samples will vary. Check to be sure that students have correctly completed all of the earlier steps in the writing process and have followed the instructions for publishing their work.

Page 37

Day 1: 1. spy; 2. Answers will vary but may include saw, noticed, or spotted. 3. Pete running into the kitchen; 4. Answers will vary. **Day 2:** 1. restroom; 2, to complete 25 math problems; 3. Answers will vary. 4. Answers will vary. **Day 3:** 1. driveway; 2. scraped; 3. loudly; 4. Answers will vary. **Day 4:** 1. (circled) normally, commonly; 2. Students from another class checked them out. 3. frustrated; 3. Answers will vary.

Page 38

1. Answers will vary. 2. quicksand; 3. (underlined) Quicksand is a deep bed of light, loose sand that is full of water. 4. Yes, on the surface, they look the same. 5A. (circled) sink; 5B. (circled) sink; 5C. (circled) float; D. (circled) float; E. (circled) float

Page 39

Day 1: 1. New York City; 2. S; 3. Sabena at the crunchy apple. 4. (underlined) at, ate; **Day 2:** 1. Orange County; 2. S; 3. The clown gave Tripp a candy can. 4. (underlined) can, cane; **Day 3:** 1. Lake Superior, United States; 2. F; 3. I want to fly my kit. 4. (underlined) kit, kite; **Day 4:** 1. Chloe, Camp Willow; 2. (circled) S; 3. Did Jared take car of his puppy? 4. (underlined) car, care

Page 40

1. Tad, Chicago, Lake Michigan; 2. Bermuda, Atlantic Ocean; 3. Michigan, Lansing; 4. F; 5. S; 6. S; 7. Wow, it is just what I wanted! 8. It is so cold! 9. (underlined) Rip; Ripe peaches are good to eat. 10. (underlined) not; Mom wrote a note to my teacher.

Page 41

Day 1: 1. Laura Ingalls Wilder; 2. writing books; 3. hardships; 4. Answers will vary. **Day 2:** 1. a shelter dug into the side of a hill; 2. Answers will vary but may include that it protected them from the weather. 3. Answers will vary but may include that it did not provide a lot of space. 4. Answers will vary. **Day 3:** 1. atlas; 2. a high fever; 3. She went to school and learned skills to help her have a better life. 4. Answers will vary. **Day 4:** 1. Land on the prairie was free, people staked a claim to live on a piece of land. 2. Answers will vary but should include a covered wagon and few possessions. 3. Answers will vary.

Page 42

1. Answers will vary. 2. One winter, food could not be delivered. 3. her daughter, Rose; 4. Answers will vary.

Page 43

Day 1: 1. Sally; 2. (circled) walked; 3. David, John, and Leo went to the beach. 4. libraries, cities; **Day 2:** 1. She, Aunt Irene, Monday; 2. (circled) runs; 3. Oh, what did they do? 4. groceries, fireflies; **Day 3:** 1. Bill, Corinna, Blair's; 2. (circled) except; 3. They swam, ate lunch, and played volleyball. 4. boys, countries; **Day 4:** 1. Aunt Irene, Culver City, California, April; 2. sits; 3. Well, what did they do with the surfboard? 4. pennies, armies

Page 44

1. To, Mackenzie; 2. She, Orange City, Tuesday, Friday; 3. Mackenzie, Nina, Paul; 4. (circled) good; 5. (circled) to; 6. (circled) accept; 7. Andrew, Clarke, and Vince took turns using the board. 8. The boys took turns floating, paddling, and riding the waves on the board. 9. monkeys; 10. ponies; 11. parties; 12. trays

Page 45

Day 1: 1. Answers will vary but should include something about forests. 2. Answers will vary. 3. a forest of redwood trees; 4. football field; **Day 2:** 1. redwood tree and a 20-story building; 2. Both are tall. 3. Answers may vary but should include trees are living things and buildings are nonliving things. 4. Estimates will vary but should be about 30 feet (arm spans of six people). **Day 3:** 1. Redwoods are tough trees. 2. thick; 3. fire, insects, disease; 4. storms, floods, fires; **Day 4:** 1. Redwoods take many years to grow. 2. They keep growing for 600 to 1,200 years. 3. Answers will vary. 4. Answers will vary.

Page 46

1. C; 2. how redwood grow so big; 3. C; 4. Tannic acid keeps pests from hurting redwood trees. 5. Their bark does not burn easily and the needles and branches that could burn easily are far above the ground. 6. C

Page 47

Day 1: The brainstorming activity should contain various ideas or words related to how dogs and snakes are alike and different. **Day 2:** The first draft should build on ideas taken from the brainstorming activity including a comparison of likenesses and differences between dogs and snakes. **Day 3:** The next draft should show improvements in clarity and cohesiveness. **Day 4:** The final draft should show proofreading marks where needed.

Page 48

The content of writing samples will vary. Check to be sure that students have correctly completed all of the earlier steps in the writing process and have followed the instructions for publishing their work.

Page 49

Day 1: 1. pelicans; 2. pouch; 3. (underlined) "A wonderful bird is a pelican; its bill will hold more than its belly can." 4. bill; **Day 2:** 1. North America is a continent. The United States is a country in North America. 2. types; 3. white pelicans and brown pelicans; 4. The white pelican lives around lakes and the brown pelican lives near oceans and gulfs. **Day 3:** 1. Brown pelicans were dying because of dirty, unsafe water. 2. safe; 3. cleaner; 4. A; **Day 4:**

1. large; 2. They are both sizeable and they both eat fish. 3. White pelicans are larger than brown pelicans, and they have different ways of catching fish. 4. Answers will vary.

Page 50
1. how pelicans fish; 2. startled; 3. a shopping bag; 4. They both fly above the water looking for fish. 5. Brown pelicans fish alone and scoop up the fish; white pelicans fish in groups and beat their wings to cause the fish to swim to the middle of the group. 6. Drawings will vary.

Page 51
Day 1: The brainstorming activity should contain three various ideas or words related to the topic sentence about friendship. **Day 2:** The first draft should build on ideas taken from the brainstorming activity related to the topic of friendship. **Day 3:** The next draft should show improvements in clarity and cohesiveness. **Day 4:** The final draft should show proofreading marks where needed.

Page 52
The content of writing samples will vary. Check to be sure that students have correctly completed all of the earlier steps in the writing process and have followed the instructions for publishing their work.

Page 53
Day 1: 1. sunken treasure; 2. excited; 3. It is exciting to think about buried treasure but it does not seem real. 4. Answers will vary. **Day 2:** 1. Kip Wagner; 2. Answers will vary depending on the current year. 3. A man in Florida found treasure. 4. an old Spanish coin; **Day 3:** 1. (circled) determined, curious; 2. Where the coin came from and what it was worth; 3. Answers will vary. 4. Kip became interested in learning more about the old coin. **Day 4:** 1. Kip learned that a ship carrying gold, silver, and jewels had sunk near the location he found the coin. 2. C; 3. Answers will vary. 4. Answers will vary.

Page 54
1. Answers will vary but should describe Kip as adventurous. 2. B; 3. A; 4. A, C, D

Page 55
Day 1: The brainstorming activity should contain various ideas or words related to the main idea about ways schools can recycle. **Day 2:** The first draft should build on ideas taken from the brainstorming activity related to the topic of recycling. **Day 3:** The next draft should show improvements in clarity and cohesiveness. **Day 4:** The final draft should show proofreading marks where needed.

Page 56
The content of writing samples will vary. Check to be sure that students have correctly completed all of the earlier steps in the writing process and have followed the instructions for publishing their work.

Page 57
Day 1: 1. skaters; 2. crying; 3. in the solar system; 4. asks how she can help; **Day 2:** 1. nice; 2. sunlight reflected from the moon's surface; 3. One of her moons has lost its ring. 4. Answers will vary. **Day 3:** 1. space; 2. quickly; 3. bright; 4. raced to Saturn and brought back a ring; **Day 4:** 1. crossed, craters; 2. Answers will vary but may include *threw* or *launched*. 3. Answers will vary. 4. fiction because planets and moons do not talk and rings from planets cannot be moved by a space officer

Page 58
1. Both passages talk about planets and moons. *The Lost Ring* is fantasy fiction; *Mars* is realistic fiction. 2. whole; 3. She changes her topic to Mars. 4. (1) Alicia's teacher tells her Mars is called the Red Planet. (2) Alicia learns that Mars is the fourth planet from the sun. (3) Alicia looks on the Internet and finds pictures of Mars. 5. because Alicia learns a lot about Mars from her research

Page 59
Day 1: The brainstorming activity should contain various descriptive ideas or words related to the main idea. **Day 2:** The first draft should build on ideas taken from the brainstorming activity. **Day 3:** The next draft should show improvements in clarity

and cohesiveness. **Day 4:** The final draft should show proofreading marks where needed.

Page 60

The content of writing samples will vary. Check to be sure that students have correctly completed all of the earlier steps in the writing process and have followed the instructions for publishing their work.

Page 61

Day 1: 1. good; 2. Answers will vary but may include delicious or yummy. 3. (circled) Nothing tastes quite as good on pancakes or waffles as maple syrup. 4. (underlined) The native people in eastern Canada made maple syrup a long time ago. Native people from the northern part of the United States made it too. **Day 2:** 1. A; 2. because it is a long process; 3. from the native people; 4. implied; **Day 3:** 1. boots; 2. sugar and water mixture from trees; 3. All three sentences in the paragraph should be underlined. 4. Answers will vary. **Day 4:** 1. ages; 2. hurt; 3. sugar maples and black maples; 4. facts

Page 62

1. a tube; 2. Answers will vary but illustrations should include a spout in the tree trunk with a bucket hanging under the spout. 3. (circled) It smells so good! But, the taste of maple syrup in the morning makes all of the work worthwhile! 4. Answers will vary, but one fact from each paragraph in the passage should be underlined. 5. Answers will vary but may include wood to make furniture or fruit to eat from fruit trees.

Page 63

Day 1: The brainstorming activity should contain various ideas or words related to the main idea. **Day 2:** The first draft should build on ideas taken from the brainstorming activity. Supportive sentences should give information that tell about the author's family. **Day 3:** The next draft should show improvements in clarity and cohesiveness. **Day 4:** The final draft should show proofreading marks where needed.

Page 64

The content of writing samples will vary. Check to be sure that students have correctly completed all of the earlier steps in the writing process and have followed the instructions for publishing their work.

94

Page 65

Day 1: 1. rough; 2. safe; 3. It belongs to a threatened species. 4. fiction, because turtles do not talk; **Day 2:** 1. fact; 2. Answers will vary, but one possible answer is to make the facts more interesting and personal. 3. Answers will vary. 4. Answers will vary but may include hide in their shells or swim away. **Day 3:** 1. enough; 2. having lots of people; 3. Answers will vary. 4. Answers will vary. **Day 4:** 1. predators; 2. prey; 3. Answers will vary. 4. No. Dogs, birds, raccoons, and crabs are also a threat to turtles.

Page 66

1. caught, captured; 2. water pollution and fishing nets; 3. Answers will vary but should indicate that the author cares for sea turtles and the environment. 4. bad or negative; 5. (1) C; (2) D; (3) A; (4) B

Page 67

Day 1: 1. *There Are Rocks in My Socks*; 2. of; 3. David asked, "What is the longest river?"; 4. their; **Day 2:** 1. *Gus Was a Friendly Ghost*; 2. off; 3. "What are you reading?" asked Mark. 4. They're; **Day 3:** 1. *The Book of Giant Stories*; 2. from; 3. "According to this book," said Jill, "geese fly the highest."; 4. there; **Day 4:** 1. *The Teeny, Tiny Witch*; 2. have; 3. "Did you know that only two types of mammals lay eggs?" asked Holly. 4. there

Page 68

1. *Exploring the World of Fossils*; 2. *The World of Insects*; 3. *Yellow Rose of Texas*; 4. have; 5. off; 6. from; 7. "Do spiders live in their webs?" asked David. 8. "Sure," replied Mark. 9. They're; 10. their

Page 69

Day 1: 1. Answers will vary but should address the word champion. 2. Bonnie Blair; 3. racing on ice skates; 4. She is the only American woman to have won five Olympic gold medals in the Winter Olympics. **Day 2:** 1. She is the youngest in a speed-skating family. She has five older brothers and sisters. 2. Answers will vary. 3. Answers will vary. 4. Answers will vary. **Day 3:** 1. She trained six days a week, always pushing herself. 2. trained; 3. France and Norway; 4. Answers will vary. **Day 4:** 1. She became famous all over the world. 2. Answers will vary. 3. Answers will vary. 4. Answers will vary.

Page 70
1. Jane Goodall; 2. Tanzania, Africa; 3. No, she had to watch them through field glasses. 4. Answers will vary, but facts should be taken from the passage. 5. Jane Goodall loved her work and was successful in helping people learn many new things about chimpanzees.

Page 71
Day 1: The brainstorming activity should list three things the author is good at. **Day 2:** The first draft should build on ideas taken from the brainstorming activity. **Day 3:** The next draft should show improvements in clarity and cohesiveness. **Day 4:** The final draft should show proofreading marks where needed.

Page 72
The content of writing samples will vary. Check to be sure that students have correctly completed all of the earlier steps in the writing process and have followed the instructions for publishing their work.

Page 73
Day 1: 1. Vasco de Balboa; 2. Spanish; 3. by ship; 4. B; **Day 2:** 1. (underlined) Balboa became a popular governor of Darien. 2. to find treasures; 3. discovering the Pacific Ocean; 4. Answers will vary. **Day 3:** 1. A new governor had replaced him. 2. He moved to a different site and built a city. 3. He built ships. 4. Yes, he made many friends. **Day 4:** 1. Pedrarias was the man who replaced Balboa as governor. 2. trying to overthrow the government; 3. guilty; 4. Answers will vary but should cite facts from the passage.

Page 74
1. the North Star; 2. C; 3. B; 4. A; 5. Answers will vary. You can look on the northern part of a map or globe.

Page 75
Day 1: The brainstorming activity should contain various ideas or words providing details or examples about three things the author is good at from Week 32. **Day 2:** The first draft should build on ideas taken from the brainstorming activity. **Day 3:**

The next draft should show improvements in clarity and cohesiveness. **Day 4:** The final draft should show proofreading marks where needed.

Page 76
The content of writing samples will vary. Check to be sure that students have correctly completed all of the earlier steps in the writing process and have followed the instructions for publishing their work.

Page 77
Day 1: 1. Answers will vary. 2. a shaking motion; 3. question; 4. B; **Day 2:** 1. three; 2. lots, several, numerous; 3. B; 4. C; **Day 3:** 1. slower and lower; 2. slower; lower; 3. higher, lower; 4. A; **Day 4:** 1. unpleasant; 2. pleasant and unpleasant; 3. (circled) chainsaw, rock music concert; 4. Sounds can be unpleasant or pleasant.

Page 78
1. No, it only gives a name. 2. He decided to become active in sports instead of getting into trouble. 3. White and black people played in separate baseball leagues. 4. being the first African American player in Major League Baseball; 5. to not fight back when people were unkind; 6. Answers will vary.

Page 79
Day 1: The brainstorming activity should restate the three things the author is good at from Week 32. **Day 2:** The first draft should build on ideas taken from the brainstorming activity and should begin with a transition word or phrase. **Day 3:** The next draft should show improvements in clarity and cohesiveness. **Day 4:** The final draft should show proofreading marks where needed.

Page 80
The content of writing samples will vary. Check to be sure that students have correctly completed all of the earlier steps in the writing process and have followed the instructions for publishing their work.

Page 81
Day 1: 1. Jose and his grandfather; 2. plant a garden to attract butterflies; 3. a butterfly garden must provide food that caterpillars like; 4. Butterflies

must eat in the adult stage; **Day 2:** 1. Delia; 2. Insects were eating her garden plants. 3. Delia want to find a natural solution; 4. they eat insect pests but do not damage a garden; **Day 3:** 1. huge masses of slowly moving ice; 2. no; 3. glaciers grew larger; 4. glaciers pick up parts of land as they move; **Day 4:** 1. (any two) Lake Superior, Lake Michigan, Lake Huron, Lake Erie, or Lake Ontario; 2. melting glaciers and rain; 3. glaciers to melt; 4. melting glaciers filling the large holes with water

Page 82
1. h; 2. ground-up plants mixed with water; 3. stems, leaves, flowers, bark, and roots; 4. B; 5. Answers will vary.

Page 83
Day 1: The brainstorming activity should list a topic and things the author knows and wants to know about the topic. In the third column the author should write information from research. **Day 2:** The first draft should build on ideas taken from the brainstorming activity with the KWL chart. **Day 3:** The next draft should show improvements in clarity and cohesiveness. **Day 4:** The final draft should show proofreading marks where needed.

Page 84
The content of writing samples will vary. Check to be sure that students have correctly completed all of the earlier steps in the writing process and have followed the instructions for publishing their work.

Page 85
Day 1: 1. soft c; 2. relatives of people who came before; 3. A; 4. Central America and southern Mexico; **Day 2:** 1. (circled) dates, invaded, overcame; 2. defended; 3. A; 4. record dates and important events; **Day 3:** 1. cycles; calendars; 2. accurate; 3. B; 4. astronomy, develop calendars; **Day 4:** 1. great; 2. 0; 3. B; 4. a symbol for zero

Page 86
1. (underlined) continues, created, customs; created; 2. ruins; 3. A; 4. A, B, C, E; 5. Mayan Indians, language, religious, customs, ruins

Page 87
Day 1: The brainstorming activity should list information about the Maya. **Day 2:** The first draft

should build on facts taken from the brainstorming activity and contain a beginning, a middle, and an ending. **Day 3:** The next draft should show improvements in clarity and cohesiveness. **Day 4:** The final draft should show proofreading marks where needed.

Page 88
The content of writing samples will vary. Check to be sure that students have correctly completed all of the earlier steps in the writing process and have followed the instructions for publishing their work.